THE HISTORY OF THE
BALTIMORE
& OHIO
AMERICA'S FIRST RAILROAD

THE HISTORY OF THE
BALTIMORE
& OHIO
AMERICA'S FIRST RAILROAD

Edited by
Timothy Jacobs

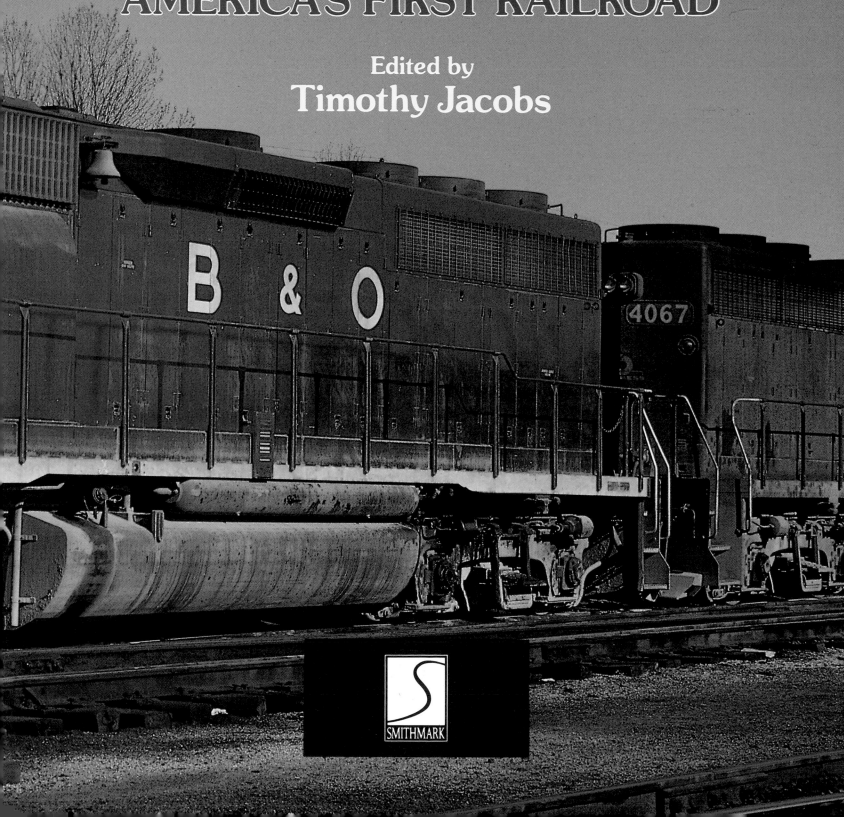

SMITHMARK

This edition published in 1995 by SMITHMARK Publishers Inc., 16 East 32nd Street New York, New York 10016

SMITHMARK books are available for bulk purchase for sales promotion and premium use. For details write or telephone the Manager of Special Sales, SMITHMARK Publishers Inc., 16 East 32nd Street, New York, NY 10016. (212) 532-6600.

ISBN 0-8317-3785-9

Reprinted 1996

Printed in China

10 9 8 7 6 5 4

PICTURE CREDITS

AGS Archives: 12, 13 (top and bottom), 18, 44, 47 (top), 75 (top)
Association of American Railroads: 28-29, 33 (bottom), 34-35, 36 (bottom), 51 (top), 58-59 (all), 64
Bison Picture Library: 49 (all), 50, 51 (bottom)
B&O Railroad Company: 22-23 (all), 26, 27 (bottom), 38 (top), 40-41, 43 (top), 46-47, 65 (all), 71, 74
B&O Railroad Museum: 14, 15, 16-17, 20 (top), 30-31, 38 (top), 40-41, 42-43, 55, 61, 70, 86 (top), 92-93, 94 (all), 101 (bottom), 113, 115, 116-117, 118-119
HL Broadbelt: 104-105
Charles A Brown: 1, 4-5, 8, 56-57, 66-67, 72-73, 75 (bottom), 76-77, 78 (all), 79, 80-81, 82-83, 84, 85, 86-87, 88-89, 90-91 (all), 95, 96-97, 101 (top), 103, 105 (top), 108-109 (all), 112 (all), 114
John B Corns, CSX Corporation: 126 (all), 127 (all)
Currier & Ives: 10-11
Dover Publications: 32, 60, 69, 100
Golden Spike Productions: 2-3, 6-7, 9, 24 (bottom), 25 (right), 27 (top), 38-39, 45, 54, 62-63, 98-99, 102 (all), 106-107, 110-111, 116 (top), 117 (top), 120 (all), 121, 122, 123, 124, 125 (all), 126 (all), 127 (all)
Library of Congress: 20-21, 24-25, 36-37, 44, 52-53
Southern Pacific Historical Collection: 19

Designed by Tom Debolski

Edited and Captioned by Timothy Jacobs

ACKNOWLEDGEMENTS

The first seven chapters of this text, up to but not including 'The Fair of the Iron Horse,' and the chapters 'The Great Depression' and 'World War II and After' were adapted from *The Baltimore and Ohio: The Story of the Railroad that Grew Up with the United States*, by Carroll Bateman, which was published by the Public Relations Department of the Baltimore & Ohio Railroad. Thanks also to CSX Transportation, Inc for valuable informational assistance concerning the latter years of the B&O's evolution.

Page 1: The traditional B&O Capital Building dome logo stands out proudly — on the nose of a B&O 2-10-2 Santa Fe type locomotive, at Hyndman, Pennsylvania in the summer of 1947.

Pages 2–3: A B&O diesel. Diesels completely replaced steam power in the 1950s. This unit, a 3000 hp EMD GP40 road switcher, was photographed at Toledo, Ohio in 1975 — near the time when B&O markings would become the stuff of memory.

These pages: A Q-4 class, 2-8-2 Mikado type steam locomotive bearing the B&O name on its tender. This loco was photographed at Wilsmere, Delaware on 4 October 1947. Note that the headlight — usually positioned at the top of the boiler on the average Q-4 — is positioned on the smokebox door of this particular locomotive, and a small emergency lamp occupies the normal headlight position.

CONTENTS

INTRODUCTION

he Baltimore & Ohio Railroad was the first common carrier chartered in the US, and the first to construct tracks specifically for the purpose of transporting passengers and freight. Endowed with an enviable list of 'firsts,' the story of the B&O is emblematic of all that is revered in American railroading.

When the B&O merged with the Chesapeake & Ohio and the Western Maryland railroads on 4 February 1963, yet another dramatic chapter of this quintessentially American story was begun. Then, in 1972–73, the B&O, the C&O and the Western Maryland adopted the Chessie System name and logo as a marketing device.

Another historic milestone was attained on 1 November 1980, when the Chessie System railroads linked their corporate future with that of the Seaboard Coast Line — also a large railroad conglomerate. This was the birth of the CSX Corporation, which is essentially a holding company for the two systems. The B&O still exists as an integral part of this massive complex — and while its traditional Capitol Building dome logo and royal blue and white company colors have passed into history, the B&O lives on in the hearts and minds of many as the embodiment of a daring tradition.

From horsepower to steam power to diesels, the B&O was always on the cutting edge of the latest locomotive technology. The mighty engines that hauled such 'crack' B&O passenger trains as the *Capitol Limited*, the *National Limited*, the *Royal Blue* and the *Cincinnatian*

were products of an intense desire to constantly improve and perfect the capabilities of locomotive power. On the freight side, when President Leonor F Loree introduced the Mallet articulated locomotive to B&O operations, the ever-problematic mounting of the Alleghenies from the West seemed to be solved. And, when the B&O used diesels on some of its express passenger trains in the 1930s, it became the first in the world to do so.

This was in marked contrast to the ways things were back in the 1820s, when the idea of building a railroad from Baltimore to the Ohio River was akin to following John Donne's advice to 'catch a falling star.' The logistics were staggering, and begat a monicker for the railroad that applied even decades later, when the Baltimore Belt Line was tunneled under that fair city. This monicker was 'The Railroad University of America,' for the problems overcome time and again by the fabled B&O involved every conceivable aspect of railroad engineering.

In the 1840s, Samuel Morse found fertile ground when he planted his telegraph wires along the B&O tracks from Baltimore to Washington. From that beginning as the home of the first telegraph line to the present day CSX Corporation research and use of fiber optics communications channels, the B&O has also always been in the front line of communications technology.

Without a doubt the most important railroad to the Union war effort during the Civil War, the B&O withstood the ravages of troops from both sides, who employed varied and effective demolition techniques to

deprive the enemy from using the railroad. And with good reason, too — the first large scale troop and equipment movements by rail were conducted on the B&O with stunning success.

Floods and fierce storms also did their worst, and time after time, the B&O rebuilt, and survived to carry freight and passengers. A mostly benevolent receivership under its powerful rival, the Pennsy, and the ravages of wartime traffic in the twentieth century added to the history of survival of the B&O.

On its own for much of the first half of this century, the B&O had a 'golden age' of prestige and respect from 1910 to 1941. These were the years of the leadership of the great B&O President, Daniel Willard. It was an era that saw the first recognitions of diesel power, and the B&O's history-making use of such. The B&O became the first railroad to use air conditioned cars. This was the age of the apex of the steam locomotive, with million-pound behemoths capable of hauling those long lines of B&O cars up steep grades, and fast passenger engines breaking record after record.

These years also included the difficult Depression years, after which came World War II, and an unprecedented rise in traffic — which meant wear and tear on B&O

Previous pages: A B&O diesel freight train — at Dayton Union Station in Ohio — headed by an EMD F7 loco with a B unit, in mid-1963. *At below left:* A B&O P-7c class, 4-6-2 Pacific type loco heads train Number 5 towards Washington in this March 1947 photo taken at Arden, Delaware, just outside of Philadelphia. *Below:* A 2250 hp B&O EMD GP30 diesel road switcher in the late 1970s.

facilities, with deferred maintenance. Therefore, the road came out of the war a bit worn, and with massive deferred debts.

The 1950s saw many railroads in dire financial trouble, and the B&O was no exception. While its mechanical operating efficiency had been vastly improved with dieselization and electronic automations of various types, traffic was down, and management found it very difficult to deal successfully with the situation. The B&O was ripe for merger. After a spirited contest between the C&O and the New York Central, the B&O was fortunate to spend a recovery period in the control of the markedly healthy C&O.

Now, both C&O and B&O are operating entities under the massive umbrella of the CSX Corporation. The B&O lives on, and thanks to the marvellous B&O Museum, which is appropriately located in a former roundhouse in Baltimore, the touch and feel of the equipment it used in bygone years is not lost to us.

The history of this great railroad is a national treasure and a monument to the growth of the nation itself. Truly, the B&O grew up with the United States — from the 'first stone laid' for the railroad on 4 July 1828, to the B&O's, and the nation's, coming of age in the twentieth century. And, just as America braces itself afresh to face the problems of a new, bold century, the B&O, too, lives on — as a vital facet in the CSX Corporation, one of the healthiest and most forward-looking transport and communications organizations in the world today.

THE B&O:
AMERICA'S FIRST RAILROAD

A Growing Nation

In 1799, Daniel Boone was 'crowded' out of the wilderness of western Virginia by neighbors living 10 miles away. In search of 'elbow room,' he moved westward to a then-lonely territory that eventually became the State of Missouri. This tendency to act on almost any impetus was indicative of the restless enterprise that would characterize the United States for much of the following four decades. America of the early nineteenth century was hardworking, eager and ambitious. Its birth pangs—and the times that had tried men's souls, in the words of Tom Paine—were past.

The nation was growing up. The 50th anniversary of the Declaration of Independence, 4 July 1826, saw Thomas Jefferson and John Adams, almost the last of the founders of the nation, near death. The original 13 states had increased to 24, with two of these located west of the Mississippi River. The United States had emphasized its independence with the War of 1812 and the Monroe Doctrine of 1823; it now sought greatness with all the impatience and vigor of its youth.

In 1827, the population exceeded 12 million. The human tide had already overflowed the Atlantic seaboard and swept westward into the rich lands beyond. Suddenly, more people were living west of the Alleghenies than had lived in the entire original 13 states during George Washington's time. That very year, 90-year-old Charles Carroll, last of the 56 signers of the Declaration of independence, was living out his days on a quiet estate near Baltimore.

Early Transportation

John Quincy Adams, the sixth President of the United States and son of the second US President, held the reigns on a nation that was rapidly forging ahead into the future. Toll roads and turnpikes took the places of Indian paths and wagon trails; the rivers and lakes were being linked with man-made canals. All attempts were being made to foster trade between the centers of population in the East and the forests and farmlands in the West.

The Atlantic Ocean was being narrowed by the clipper ship and the steamship. The *Curacao*, first sea-going vessel to be powered by steam alone, crossed the Atlantic in April, 1827. The commodities from the western US would help to increase the flow of trade with Europe.

Americans were coming to realize that their future lay in the development of their country's vast natural resources, many of which were close at hand in the great valley of the Mississippi. The big problem was transportation—how to bring these commodities to the cities of the eastern US, where they could be processed for market and for export. One solution of this problem was to secure a good means of transportation between the East Coast and the banks of the wide and deep Ohio River. The Ohio was navigable from its junction with the Mississippi in the Midwest to as far as Pittsburgh in the East. Once linked with the Ohio, the seaports of the East Coast could be certain that the natural riches of the West would flow to them in abundance.

The Erie Canal, eight years in construction at the then staggering cost of $7,600,000, opened on 26 October

Previous page: A Currier & Ives print, featuring an early passenger train. During the tenure of President John Quincy Adams *(above)*, intense intercity trade competition in the eastern US led to the chartering of the B&O, an act that was to portend the demise of canal operations such as that at *(below right)*. *Above right, both:* Pre-railroad overland transportation vehicles.

1825. The rich cargoes from the West, towed from Lake Erie to New York City, were filling the pockets of Manhattan merchants. The golden success of the Erie Canal initiated a plague of 'canal fever' that was combined with much dishonest or careless financing. Wild promises of profits were made.

In the days of the toll roads, Baltimore fared well in the competition for western trade, and her seaport flourished. But now, in the third decade of the nineteenth century, the city of 80,000 saw itself losing out. The Erie Canal carried many of the western products into New York. Other extensive canal works were underway in Pennsylvania, and these would draw still more of the trade away from Baltimore and into Philadelphia. Baltimore had a great natural harbor, and her merchants hoped to make their city a great export-import center. But the only links Baltimore had with the West were the inefficient toll roads and turnpikes. True, the National Road to Wheeling, on the Ohio, fed into Maryland's Frederick Pike, and that in turn led into Baltimore, but the roads were hopelessly inadequate. Canal fever gripped the Baltimoreans, too. They wanted a navigable waterway to the West to assure their prosperity.

At first, Baltimoreans thought that the newly chartered Chesapeake & Ohio Canal was the answer to their problem. But they were dismayed to find that the canal would end on the Potomac River near Washington, and that its trade would bypass Baltimore.

Among the more far-sighted Baltimoreans were Philip E Thomas, a Quaker merchant who in 1826 was President of the National Mechanics Bank of Baltimore, and

George Brown, a Director of the same bank. Evan Thomas, brother of Philip, returned from England in 1826 to give a glowing account of a new idea in transportation—a 'rail road.' He had studied the details of the Stockton and Darlington, the first English railroad designed for general freight and passenger service.

The First American Railroad

William Brown, a member of the British Parliament, also wrote to his American brother George, the bank director, about the English railways, which then were being considered as a means of general transportation: the Liverpool and Manchester Railway was organized in 1826 for the public service, and construction of tracks and experiments with rolling stock and motive power were under way in 1826.

Philip E Thomas and George Brown became convinced that a railroad was the solution to Baltimore's transportation problem. On 12 February 1827, they invited 25 other businessmen to a meeting at Brown's home 'to take into consideration the best means of restoring to the City of Baltimore that portion of the western trade which has lately been diverted from it . . . ' They interested the others in the idea of transportation by rail, and a sub-committee was appointed to investigate the details.

The sub-committee's report spoke glowingly of 'the immense commerce which lies within our grasp to the West, provided we have the enterprise to profit by the advantages which our local situation gives us . . . Baltimore lies 200 miles nearer to the navigable waters of the West (principally, the Ohio and the Mississippi Rivers) than New York, and about 100 miles nearer to them than Philadelphia, to which may be added the important fact that the easiest, and by far the most practicable route through the ridges of the mountains . . . is along the depression formed by the Potomac.'

Means of developing routes to the West were discussed, and turnpikes were admitted to be out of date. The English canals, popular as they had been, were proving unable to handle all of the commodities offered to them for quick transport. The report went on:

'Railroads had, upon a limited scale, been used in several places in England and Wales for a number of years, and had, in every instance, been found fully to answer the purposes required . . . The idea of applying them upon a more extended scale appears, however, only recently to have been suggested in that country . . . So decided have been their advantages over turnpike roads, and even canals, that already 2000 miles of them are actually completed or in a train of rapid progress in Great Britain . . . Nor has there been one instance in which they have not fully answered the most sanguine expectations of their projectors . . . It is the opinion of many judicious and practical men there 'that these roads will, for heavy transportation, supersede canals as effectually as canals have superseded the turnpike roads.'

The recommendation that a double-track railroad be constructed between Baltimore and the Ohio River was adopted unanimously, and the enthusiastic general committee immediately asked the legislature of Maryland for permission to incorporate 'The Baltimore & Ohio Rail Road Company.' Thus began the first railroad—meaning an incorporated common carrier, using vehicles that run on tracks, offering freight and passenger schedules on a regular basis—to be chartered and built in America.

The company's charter, which served as a model for many other early railroads, was drawn up by John Van Lear McMahon, a young Baltimore lawyer and a member of the state legislature. The charter was approved on 28 February 1827. Shortly thereafter, stock was put on sale in Baltimore, and nearby Frederick and Hagerstown. So completely had the idea captured the popular imagination, that the initial offering of shares was oversub-

Above: A party surveying for the first segment of the B&O. The building of the B&O was a difficult task, entailing practically every engineering problem known to man. Thus, the B&O was known as 'The Railroad University of America.' *At far right:* The laying of the first stone of the B&O Railroad, with Charles Carroll, the last surviving signer of the Declaration of Independence, manning the spade with which he broke the earth for the project.

scribed; the State of Maryland itself subscribed to $500,000 worth. Mr Thomas was named President of the corporation; George Brown its treasurer.

To assure expert advice in supervising the rail construction, the new company hired the most prominent engineers of the day, including Colonel Stephen H Long, of the US Army engineers; Jonathan Knight, former public works engineer for the State of Pennsylvania; and Major George W Whistler, also of the Army engineers, who was to become the father of the famous painter, James McNeill Whistler. The United States Government detailed several other engineers from the Army Topographical Corps to assist in surveying the line.

They went to work at once to study possible routes. Soon, President Thomas was able to assure the stockholders that construction of the railroad was entirely possible from an engineering standpoint. There were several possible routes to the Potomac River, but a route following the valley of the Patapsco River and then the depression carved out by Bush Creek to Point of Rocks on the banks of the Potomac, was deemed best. Proceeding further from Point of Rocks, the route lay within the narrow valley of the Potomac River to Cumberland. While construction of the road was proceeding this far, other surveys would decide the location of the line west of Cumberland.

The First Stone Laid

Stone blocks were often used in early railroad construction, much the same way that the now-standard wooden ties are, to support the rails — wooden ties were also used, but had yet to demonstrate their overall superiority to the 'stones.' The first stone of the B&O was laid in Baltimore on the Fourth of July, 1828, against the colorful background of a mammoth civic celebration. The Chesapeake and Ohio Canal was begun that same day at Georgetown, DC. Such events were glorious affairs in those days, but the excited Baltimoreans were determined that nothing would outshine the beginning of their own railroad. For the Baltimore & Ohio Railroad was a community enterprise — most every citizen had bought a share of stock. And so the people made the ceremony a memorable one.

The day dawned fair to find thousands of visitors from the surrounding countryside on hand. Altogether, more than 50,000 people were present. A procession of floats representing all of the trades and industries of the city, as well as the agricultural pursuits of Maryland, paraded to Mount Clare, James Carroll's estate on the edge of the town, which was to be the site for the stone-laying. There were blacksmiths, farmers, planters, millers, weavers, cordwainers, tanners, carpenters, painters, masons, bricklayers, victuallers, bakers, tailors, hatters, and scores of others. The ceremony was in the charge of the Grand Lodge of Masons of the State of Maryland. The venerable Charles Carroll of Carrollton spaded the first earth, but US President Adams was not present. He was assisting at the celebration of the C&O Canal, which he mistakenly believed to be of greater importance.

The day — and the night that followed — were complete with prayer, oratory, band music, gift-giving, dining, toasting and other entertainment. Inside the first stone were deposited a copy of the B&O charter, newspapers of the day, and a scroll which read:

'This stone is deposited in commemoration of the commencement of the Baltimore & Ohio Railroad, a work of deep and vital interest to the American people. Its accomplishment will confer the most important benefits upon this nation, by facilitating its commerce, diffusing and extending its social intercourse, and perpetuating the happy Union of these confederated states.'

When he finished his honorary task, Charles Carroll turned to a friend and said: 'I consider this among the most important acts of my life, second only to my signing of the Declaration of Independence, if even it be second to that.'

Both of these judgments were borne out by history. For these United States of America grew physically and economically strong, helped by the Baltimore & Ohio and many other great railroads which bound them together.

On 7 July 1828, the engineers set out to determine the exact or 'definitive' location of the tracks from Baltimore to Ellicott's Mills, 13 miles west of the city. Contractors were asked to bid on the grading and bridge construction, and by October all of the successful bidders were at work.

Meanwhile, $4 million dollars had been subscribed to the company, but it was almost immediately realized that much more would be needed. A request to the federal government for a million dollar subscription of stock was blocked through the opposition of General CF Mercer, President of the C&O Canal Company. Mercer was also chairman of the roads and canals committee of the US House of Representatives.

Construction Commences

Despite lack of money and many unexpected construction difficulties, the railroad construction moved ahead steadily. Mr Thomas, in his third annual report on 12 October 1829, announced that 25 miles of the grading was complete.

At about the same time, the laying of the first rails began at Mount Clare, the terminus of the railroad in Baltimore. By 22 December, enough rail was laid for officials and distinguished visitors to make experimental rides in a horse-drawn coach. These rides attracted so much interest that on 7 January 1830, in response to public demand, the Baltimore & Ohio commenced operations, becoming the first railroad in the United States to carry revenue passengers. These passengers were taken on excursion trips from the Baltimore terminal on Pratt

Street to Carrollton Viaduct which was then being built over Gwynn's Falls, west of Baltimore. This great stone arch, 80 feet between inside faces, supported even the B&O's heaviest locomotives well into the twentieth century.

Within a few months, rails were laid all the way to Ellicott's Mills (now Ellicott City, Maryland), and on 24 May 1830, this 13 and one-half miles of road was put into service. From the very beginning, the railroad found itself unable to handle all of the passengers and freight offered for transportation. Additional cars had to be built hurriedly. During the four months of June, July, August and September, the young railroad, with only a few horse-powered cars, earned $20,000 in gross receipts.

National conditions were changing; indeed they had already changed. The era of 'good feeling' had passed with the election in 1828 of Andrew Jackson, 'The Son of the West.' Regional differences rising between the West, the Northeast and the South were producing a troublesome economic/political milieu which would lend scant encouragement to the furthering of a great enterprise. Nevertheless, the railroad builders forged ahead.

TRACKS TO THE OHIO

Early Steam Locomotives

When the tiny *Tom Thumb* puffed successfully down the tracks of the Baltimore & Ohio in 1830, it became the first American-built locomotive to operate on an American railroad. But it was not the first steam locomotive in history. The story of man's effort to design a steam engine-capable of moving itself overland begins before the founding of the B&O, and in fact, long before the dawning of the nineteenth century. It goes back a hundred years before the American Revolution, to the time when the Great Fire of London still was fresh in the memories of many.

In 1680, Sir Isaac Newton sketched plans for a steam engine designed to move on land, the first record of such a machine. From that time on, inventive minds pursued the idea, for such motive power had obvious advantages: it combined the mobility of a horse or mule with the greater power, speed and endurance of a machine. Newton's engine, never built, was to be propelled by the force of a jet of steam blown to the rear through a nozzle. The first steam engine to move overland successfully under its own power was built by Nicholas Joseph Cugnot, a French military engineer, nearly a century later, in 1769. Cugnot's engine was designed for hauling cannon, but it met with a serious accident on the streets of Paris and the inventor went to prison for his pains.

In the coal mines of eighteenth-century England, stationary steam engines came into use to operate winches that pulled the heavy coal cars up inclined tracks by ropes. Horse power was used on the level tracks. Similar stationary engines were planned by early B&O engineers to pull the horse-drawn trains up the steep slopes of central Maryland. These slope-traversing systems were called 'inclined planes,' and, while they greatly facilitated the negotiating of mountainous countryside, they were quite dangerous, as proper braking systems for the cars were some years in the making, and accidents often happened.

An Englishman, Richard Trevithick, who had built high-pressure stationary steam engines for the English mines, turned his efforts in 1801 to constructing a steam-powered vehicle that would move on ordinary toll roads. Three years later, in conjunction with Andrew Vivian, he developed a steam engine designed expressly for railroads, and it served as the model for many later designs.

Other engines were developed, each with new refinements. William Hedley of England proved, with a hand-driven machine in 1812, that smooth driving wheels would adhere to smooth rails. Forced draught to guarantee a continuous hot fire was first employed by a French inventor in 1827. The 'Rainhill Trials,' conducted in England by the Liverpool & Manchester Railway in 1829, brought forth five improved engines. Outstanding among these was Robert Stephenson's *Rocket*, winner of the 500-pound (Sterling) first prize.

The 'Road of Rails'

The first record of a 'road of rails' dates all the way back to 1602, more than two centuries before the enterprising group of Baltimoreans banded together to

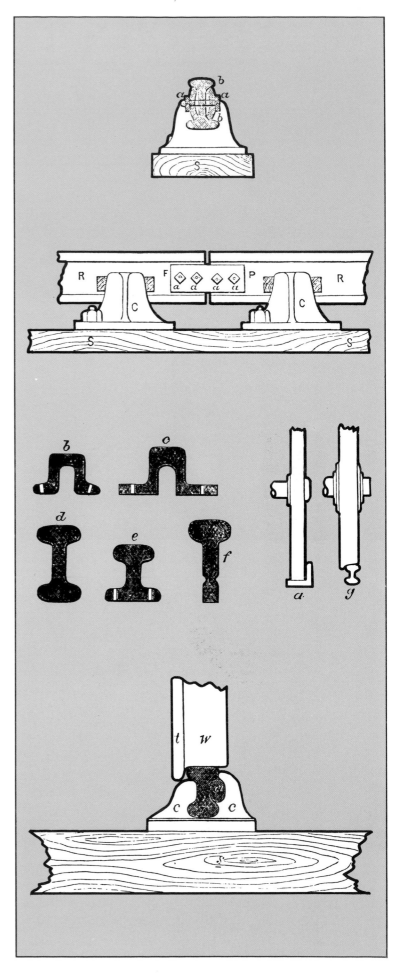

Previous page: The original *Atlantic*, a nineteenth century B&O 'grasshopper' type loco, pulls a string of reproduction Imlay Coach cars at the Fair of the Iron Horse in 1927 (see page 89). *Above:* An illustration of various early rails that were used on the 'road of rails.' The first vehicles on such were horsecars.

British railroad activity in the 1820s inspired American enterpreneurs; especially admired were the locomotive designs that came out of Great Britain and Europe. One of the first outstanding steam locomotive designs was Robert Stephenson's *Rocket (below)*, which won the Liverpool & Manchester Railway's Rainhill Locomotive Trials, held in Great Britain in 1829.

join their city to the Ohio River by rail. This first recorded railroad was merely a clever improvement on a dirt road—on which coal was hauled in carts from an English mine to the dock of a nearby canal.

To build this railroad, the roadway had been leveled, and on it were laid oak cross-ties at three-foot intervals. Upon the ties were laid two parallel strips of wood, or 'rails,' sufficiently broad to provide a smooth, even surface for the cart wheels. So effective were these rails in reducing the friction on the wheels that a horse or mule was able to pull two and one-half times as much weight as it could without the 'railroad.'

There was, however, a tendency for the wooden rails to wear through quickly, and iron plates were laid atop them to lessen the need for replacements. Additional improvements came gradually. The wooden rails overlaid with iron plates gave way in 1738 to cast iron rails laid directly upon the crossties. When these were found to frequently break under the weight of a heavily-laden coal cart, the idea of dispersing the weight by the use of a train of carts, or 'cars,' was born.

Thus about 1768, instead of placing all of the burden in one large cart, the miners divided the coal among several smaller carts, distributing the weight more widely over the length of the rails. About the same time, cast iron wheels had been invented to take the place of less durable wooden wheels, but the metal wheels did not come into general use until an efficient brake could be devised for them. In the meantime, the grooved rail had been outmoded by the wheel with a flange, which better served the purpose of keeping the vehicle on the track.

ROCKET.

A new 'malleable iron' rail was invented in 1805 to replace the brittle cast iron type. The malleable iron rail was too narrow to be used generally (to make it wider would have been difficult and expensive), but an improvement upon it in 1820 combined a broad top surface based on a narrow, strong upright section. This was the forerunner of the modern I-shaped heavy-duty railroad rail.

The first tracks laid by the Baltimore & Ohio Railroad were made in three styles. These included wooden rails or 'stringers' laid upon wooden crossties or 'sleepers.' Iron straps were fixed atop the wooden rails. A second type was made up of iron rails affixed directly to stone blocks or laid in two parallel rows beneath the rail. Still a third type employed iron rails fixed to wooden 'stringers,' these in turn being laid upon stone blocks for support.

The cost of building the road with wooden cross-ties

Below: A survey map of the various routes proposed for the B&O. *At right,* early motive power — a B&O horsecar at Relay, Maryland.

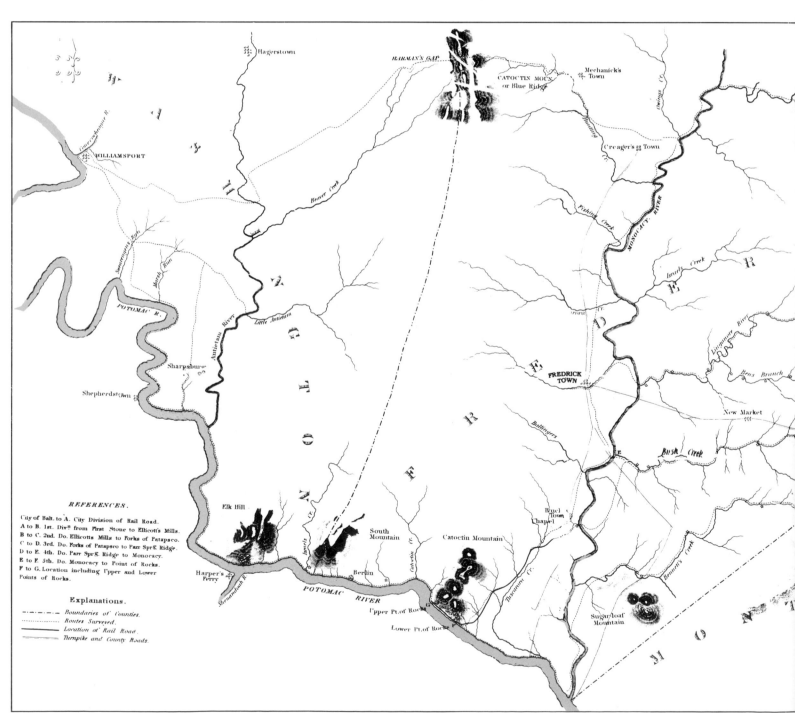

REFERENCES.

City of Balt. to A. City Division of Rail Road.
A to B. 1st. Divⁿ from First Stone to Ellicott's Mills.
B to C. 2nd. Do. Ellicotts Mills to Forks of Patapsco.
C to D. 3rd. Do. Forks of Patapsco to Parr Sprg. Ridge.
D to E. 4th. Do. Parr Sprg. Ridge to Monocacy.
E to F. 5th. Do. Monocacy to Point of Rocks.
F to G. Location including Upper and Lower Points of Rocks.

Explanations.

Boundaries of Counties.
Routes Surveyed.
Location of Rail Road.
Turnpike and County Roads.

and iron-topped stringers stood at more than $4400 per mile, even in the 1830s. Nevertheless, it proved to be the least expensive style, and the easiest to maintain. It has developed into the type of rail in use today, for, while the wooden stringers have disappeared, the iron plates have grown into the I-shaped rail. Today, in order to bear the heavier and faster trains, the rails are made of specially processed steel, and they weigh as much as 152 pounds per yard. The crossties, to which these heavy rails are fixed by steel spikes, are treated to protect them against the moisture of the earth and have a life of up to 30 years. Regardless of these improvements, the basic principle of rail construction is the same as it was more than 150 years ago.

Early Motive Power

In the beginning, all of the Baltimore & Ohio trains were horse-powered. Usually rented from stagecoach companies, the horses were well cared for and carefully groomed, and were not required to pull a car for more than six or seven miles at one time. The horses were satisfactory for the first 13-mile route of the B&O between Baltimore and Ellicott's Mills, but the managers of the road foresaw difficulties if horse power had to be used all the way to the Ohio River. Therefore, they were interested in the English experiments with steam locomotives. Soon after news of the Rainhill Trials reached America, the Baltimore & Ohio began testing a locomotive of American design. This was the *Tom Thumb*, constructed in 1829 by Peter Cooper, a New York merchant, inventor and philanthropist. After many difficulties, the little engine made a successful round trip between Baltimore and Ellicott's Mills in August, 1830, running at speeds of up to 18 miles an hour and pushing a car carrying 23 passengers. The B&O engineer Ross Winans reported:

'. . . Today's experiments must, I think, establish

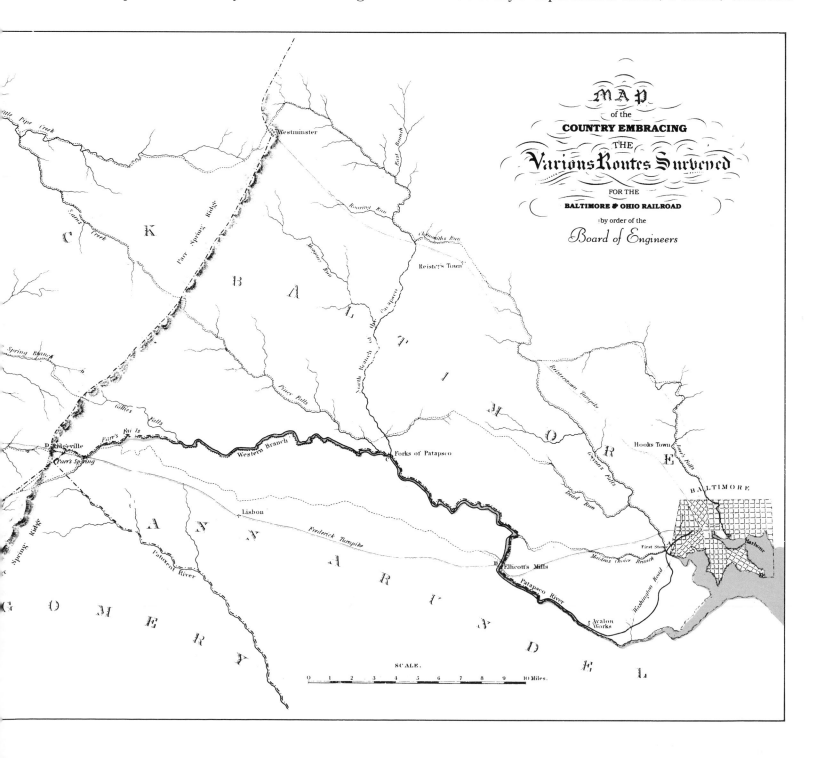

PETER COOPER'S "TOM THUMB" 1829-30 BALTIMORE & OHIO R. R.

beyond a doubt the practicability of using locomotive steam power on the Baltimore & Ohio Railroad for the conveyance of passengers and goods at such speeds and with such safety (when compared with other modes) as will be perfectly satisfactory to all parties concerned and with such economy as must be highly flattering to the interests of the company.'

For some time Cooper's engine was employed in pulling cars of distinguished visitors. On one occasion, the *Tom Thumb* engaged in an impromptu race with a horse-drawn car. Although the engine came in second—because the belt that operated the blower for the firedraft slipped off its pully—still it proved itself, for the duration of its run, to be faster than the horse.

The *Tom Thumb* was, however, an experimental model, and was not practical for regular service. Two other methods of motive power were tested, with but little success. One was a car carrying a horse which walked upon a treadmill geared to the wheels. The other, a car with a sail like a ship, appropriately named the *Aeolus*, attracted considerable attention. The Russian Ambassador to the United States, after a thrilling ride on the *Aeolus*, obtained a model which he sent to the Czar, and this encouraged renewed interest in the building of a railroad between St Petersburg and Moscow.

The B&O, in January of 1831, offered a purchase prize of $4000 for the best steam engine to be presented for a contest on June 1 of that same year. The specifications given were for a coal burning engine weighing less than three and one-half tons, and capable of pulling a 15-ton load at 15 miles per hour. Despite the relatively large prizes for the time (the second prize was $3500), only four engines were submitted: the *James*, built in New York; the *Costell*, from Philadelphia; the *Johnson*, a Baltimore product; and the *York*, built by a clever Pennsylvania watchmaker, Phineas Davis, at the town

Peter Cooper's *Tom Thumb*, built in 1829, was the first locomotive built in America, and was also the B&O's first. *At left:* A painting of *Tom Thumb's* race against a B&O horsecar in August 1830. *Below: Tom Thumb*, at the Fair of the Iron Horse (see page 89).

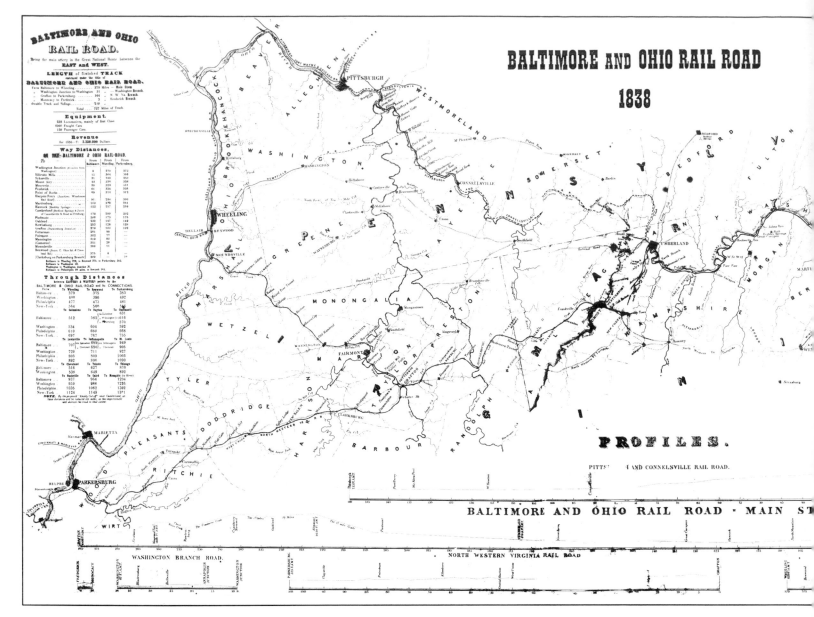

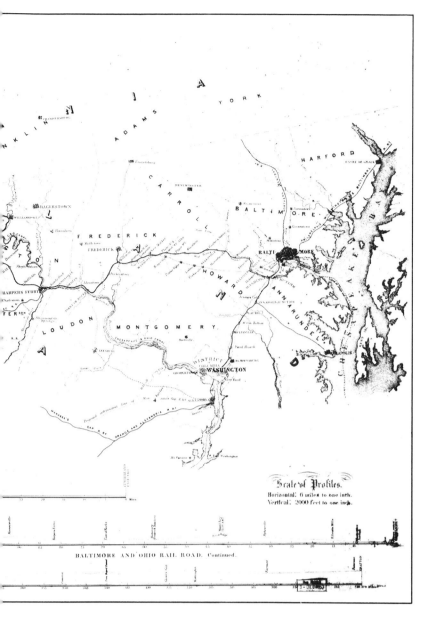

Above: An Imlay coach car of the kind used by the B&O in 1831. Elegant as it appears, it shares its undercarriage design with the rugged four wheel barrel car of the same era at *below far left. At left:* A map of the B&O and contingent lines made in 1838.

for which his engine was named. Davis had to dismantle his engine and trundle it in an ox-cart down the turnpike to Baltimore. The contest, postponed until June 27, in the futile hope of garnering more entries, finally was conducted without the glamor and fanfare that had heralded the Rainhill Trials in England. The *York* was found to be best; it did much better than the specifications required.

The chief worry of the B&O Directors had been that a locomotive large and powerful enough to be practical would not be able to negotiate the railroad's sharpest curves, built on a minimum radius of 400 feet. The *York* sped around the sharpest turns at 15 miles per hour, and on the straightaway it achieved the unheard-of speed of 30 miles per hour without mishap. A survey showed that locomotives such as the *York* could be operated for about $16.00 a day, whereas the same amount of work done by horse power would cost about $33.00.

In July, the Baltimore & Ohio introduced a regular passenger train powered by the *York*, and the capable Phineas Davis became for a short time chief mechanical engineer of the company. The *York* performed commendably, hauling at one time as many as five cars filled with passengers. It remained in daily service for many, many years, pulling trains on the 80-mile round trip between Baltimore and Frederick, Maryland.

By 1835, the Baltimore & Ohio was operating seven locomotives, not counting the already obsolete *Tom Thumb*, and it had 44 passenger cars and 1078 'burthen,' or 'burden' cars, as freight cars then were called. Improvements soon were being made in the passenger cars, which at first had been modeled after the horse-drawn stage coaches. The versatile engineer, Ross Winans, who had become associated with the B&O shortly after its organization, produced in 1831 the first eight-wheel passenger coach. This had two 'trucks,' or a set of four wheels at each end of the car. It was named the *Columbus*. This truck arrangement permitted cars of greater length than was then customary to go around sharp curves without derailing, and passenger car of a much roomier type could be built. Winans also was responsible for many other early developments in railroad car design, including the immensely important idea of axles that turned with their wheels, which is still a basic principle of railroad car design.

Phineas Davis was killed in an accident involving one of his own engines on 27 September 1835. The Mount Clare Shops in Baltimore, which Davis had built in 1833, and which were the first railroad shops in America, which he had built in 1833, were taken over by the partnership of Ross Winans and George Gillingham. Eventually, the company itself took over these historic

shops, which eventually grew to many times their original size. In them, great steam (and a century later, diesel-electric) locomotives, passenger and freight cars and other railroad equipment were repaired and sometimes built entirely new.

The power and speed of the locomotives improved steadily; more and more cars were added to the trains. The steam engine gave yet one more impressive display of its power on 12 September 1836, when the Maryland volunteer militia was carried from Baltimore to Washington to commemorate the anniversary of the Battle of North Point. One engine pulled cars containing 300 troops, with their arms and equipment, the largest number of persons ever carried in one train to that time. The remaining 700 troops with all their equipment were moved in three other trains. The demonstration indicated to military as well as railroad men that, in time of war the railroads would constitute the quickest and best means of transporting military units and their equipment.

Expansion

By April of 1832, the track of the B&O had snaked its way westward as far as Point of Rocks, Maryland, on the banks of the Potomac River. The railroad now began bringing the produce from the farmlands of the Potomac Valley into the city. And from Point of Rocks — as well as from Frederick, Maryland, which was linked to the main line by a branch road — many other products were being shipped to Baltimore in mounting volumes: lumber, firewood, granite, coal and more. One of the chief items of freight was flour. About 500 barrels of flour per day (in

The *Atlantic*, shown *above*, had a service life of 60 years altogether. *Above right:* The Thomas Viaduct on the Washington Branch — an early B&O engineering feat. *Below right:* The B&O's Mount Clare Station, built in 1829, was the world's first passenger station.

a good period) moved into Baltimore.

But now the B&O ran head-on into a legal battle that stalled its westward advance for more than a year. In January 1832, the Maryland Court of Appeals ordered the railroad not to use the land it had acquired beyond Point of Rocks until the Chesapeake & Ohio Canal was located. The reasoning behind this decision was as follows. If the two projects were not planned together, there was the possibility of room being left for the railroad once the canal was laid out — because of the narrowness of the Potomac Valley on the Maryland side. Eventually, the Maryland Legislature effected a compromise, and in 1833 the work went ahead rapidly. By the end of 1834, the railroad had reached Harper's Ferry, where the Shenandoah joins the Potomac.

At this point, a unique S-shaped bridge was built across the Potomac, to connect the B&O with the Winchester & Potomac Railway, which ran down into the Shenandoah Valley. This opened a new trade channel, and the freight haulage of the B&O increased correspondingly. Both passenger and freight receipts now greatly exceeded expectations, though the railroad still was far from the Ohio River.

Tracks to Washington and Other Advances

In 1833, the Maryland Assembly had approved a railroad to Washington, and this Washington branch, connecting with the B&O main line at Relay, was opened in

1835. The first locomotive to enter Washington was the *Atlantic*, on 24 August of that year. But the formal dedication of the new Washington line took place the following day when four 'grasshopper' type locomotives — the *George Washington*, the *John Adams*, the *Thomas Jefferson* and the *James Madison* — puffed into the nation's Capital, each pulling four or five cars and altogether bringing 1000 passengers from Baltimore on the initial trip. The importance of the occasion was such that President Jackson dismissed his cabinet for the day, in order to watch the first train come into the station at the foot of Capitol Hill.

One outstanding feature of the new 'branch' was a great granite bridge built on a curve with eight magnificent arches over the Patapsco River. Designed by Benjamin H Latrobe, it was named the Thomas Viaduct, in honor of the B&O's first President. Like the Carrollton Viaduct over Gwynn's Falls, it was destined to serve the B&O well into the twentieth century. Altogether, the first rail connection between Baltimore and the national capital was a success, serving an average of 200 passengers daily in its early years.

President Thomas retired in 1836 because of poor health. When Louis McLane took over the Presidency at the end of the year, the B&O was in deteriorating physical condition — particularly the stretch of track between Mount Clare and Ellicott City. McLane's first move was to rebuild completely this early line. During his second year, he eliminated the dangerous inclined planes over Parr's Ridge near Mount Airy, where winches had assisted in pulling the cars uphill. A new stretch of track was built surmounting the ridge at a more gradual grade, so that the locomotives could make better time, since the time-consuming procedures involved with the old incline planes were no longer necessary.

That same year, the B&O was the first US railroad to secure a government contract — to become effective on 1 January of 1838 — to carry mail on its regular trains. Despite the physical plant improvements and the contract, McLane was faced with many troubles. Surveys showed that $9.5 million more was needed to build the line west from Harper's Ferry to Wheeling, where the connection would at last be made to the Ohio River. Virginia (West Virginia as a state in its own right was not to become a reality until 1863) subscribed to $1 million of additional stock, but the railroad was in serious financial straits despite this new subscription (and others from Maryland and Baltimore).

On to the Ohio River

McLane went to London to raise money, and the construction went ahead. The tracks reached Cumberland on 5 November 1842. Some 25 days later, the B&O operated a special locomotive from Washington to Cumberland in five hours and 50 minutes — approximately *half* the time that had been expected for this 170-mile run. But McLane was impatient to push on, on to the Ohio! He reported as follows to the Board of Directors in 1843:

'When Baltimore can communicate with St Louis and New Orleans with equal certainty at a shorter distance and at less cost than Philadelphia, New York and Boston, she may then — and not before — hope successfully to

contend with these cities for the western trade. Then and not before, her wharves may be lined with foreign ships and steamers, and she may become the mart of an extensive domestic and foreign trade.'

The legislative and engineering difficulties began to ease when, in 1846, Pennsylvania granted a charter to the Pittsburgh & Connellsville Railroad, which would link the B&O with Pittsburgh. And the Virginia legislature renewed, for the second time, its permission for continuation of the railroad to Wheeling. Even so, McLane had to visit Europe again to borrow more money.

He returned in October of 1846, to find that the revenues of the company were exceeding $650,000 a year, and he set about reorganizing the railroad into three departments — a practice then in vogue with railroads in England, as it was said to increase an organization's operating efficiency. These departments were headed by the Master of the Road, who was responsible

for the all things having to do with the railroad's right-of-way; the Master of Machinery, who was responsible for the railroad's rolling stock; and the Master of Transportation, whose responsibilities included the movement of traffic, the establishment of rates and the securing of passengers and freight.

The B&O forged steadily ahead. Unfortunately for McLane, his Herculean efforts had tired him out, and he had to give up the Presidency. Thomas Swann became President of the B&O in 1848, and he set out to complete the line to the Ohio at once, regardless of cost and difficulty. Within 14 months, 165 miles of new railroad were under construction, and by June of 1851, the line had stretched 28 miles beyond Cumberland.

Miles of rugged mountain country lay between Cumberland and Wheeling. Eleven tunnels had to be drilled, 113 bridges had to be constructed, and hundreds of fills and cuts had to be made. When tunneling delays threatened

The *Atlantic* was built according to the long-pushrod grasshopper design, which was typical of several early B&O locomotives (see text). Shown *above*, the long-lived *Atlantic* on an exhibition run.

to prolong the work, temporary bypass tracks were sometimes 'switchbacked' up the steep hills, or routed via lengthy and roundabout detours.

On 22 June 1852, the road reached the Monongahela River at Fairmont, Virginia (now West Virginia), 71 miles short of Wheeling. Track laying continued at a furious pace, and on Christmas Eve of that year, the last spike was driven at Roseby's Rock, 18 miles east of Wheeling. In addition, trackage had been laid eastward *from* Wheeling. On the first of January 1853, the first train entered Wheeling, and the B&O had reached the Ohio River at last — but there was much work to be done, even still. The time from Baltimore to Wheeling for passenger trains was set at 16 hours, a trip that had previously taken several days by horse or stagecoach.

CINCINNATI AND ST LOUIS

The 1840s

The fifth decade of the nineteenth century was a tumultuous period. While the tide of humanity had swept overland toward the Pacific Coast, other adventurers had shipped out via Cape Horn. California was being very rapidly —and heavily—settled. Therefore, the nation's West Coast was being civilised, and with the East Coast already well-populated, the area in between—the Midwest, the Mountains and the Great Plains—was the next great area to be claimed by the 'white man.' The Mormons, persecuted in Missouri and Illinois, were moving westward in an historic trek, to settle finally in Utah. Battles with Indians raged, as settlers and prospectors rushed into the wilderness. With the discovery of gold at Sutter's Mill in California, the Gold Rush of 1849 began.

In the field of science and invention, this decade was rich indeed. Dr Crawford W Long of Georgia initiated the use of anesthetics; Samuel Morse invented the telegraph key and code system, and also built the first telegraph line; Elias Howe patented the sewing machine; Richard Hoe invented the rotary printing press; and William Kelly, of Kentucky, developed the blast furnace method of making steel.

New territories of vast size were added to the United States. In the 1840s, the lower continental US (minus Alaska) had grown nearly to its present size, except for a small area to be obtained from Mexico in 1853. Texas, which obtained its independence from Mexico in 1836,

came into the Union in 1845; part of it later became part of the states of New Mexico, Colorado and Wyoming. The war with Mexico began in 1846, and when it was over, Mexico ceded to the United States another half-million square miles which eventually became the states of California, Nevada, Utah, Arizona, New Mexico and part of Colorado.

The railroads of America, which in 1840 totalled just 2818 miles of track, were greatly affected by these many developments. Territorial expansion accelerated the building of railroads to the extent that, within this one decade, the total of US trackage was more than tripled. By 1850, there were 9021 miles of railroad track, and by 1860, more than 30,000 miles, all totaled.

Innovations and Advances

New scientific developments were in some cases also closely connected with railroading. Kelly's blast furnace process of making steel, duplicated and perfected by Henry Bessemer in England, would have its definite impact upon the physical plant of every railroad in the US: the superior steel produced by the blast furnace and the Bessemer converter would go toward, among other things, making higher-quality rails for higher-speed and heavier trains. These new rails naturally also meant greater safety for passengers and crews, as they were far more durable, and less likely to buckle under stress than their predecessors.

Another invention of the period was heartily welcomed

Previous page: The 4-4-0 American type locomotive *William Mason*, built in the 1850s. *At left:* An illustration of the *Cumberland*, a B&O 'mud-digger' (see also page 98). *Above:* Historic Ellicott City Station, 13 miles from Baltimore. *At right:* An early dining car.

by rail passengers; the first dining cars to appear on an American railroad, the so-called 'refectory cars,' were introduced on the B&O in 1843. Heretofore, passenger trains made extremely hasty stops (when they stopped at all) at hotels along the line, where passengers quickly purchased their meals. Some preferred to carry their own lunches. The dining car was an advance, indeed.

Samuel Morse's invention also was to become of great value to all railroads. Morse secured permission for his 'Magnetic Telegraph Company' to build an experimental line along the Baltimore & Ohio right-of-way between Baltimore and Washington in 1843. At the B&O's Mount Clare Shops, a special machine was designed to plow a trench and bury a lead-pipe containing the telegraph wires in one operation. However, after the conduit had been laid from Mount Clare to Relay, late in 1843, rocky ground forced a change for part of the line to the (eventually) standard method of stringing the wire from wooden poles. When it was discovered that the wire inside the conduit had not been properly insulated, the entire line was restrung on on the above-ground poles. In the spring of 1844, Morse installed two sets of instruments — one in the Supreme Court Chamber in Washington and the other in the Pratt Street Station of the Baltimore & Ohio in Baltimore.

On 24 May 1844, the world's first telegraph message, 'What Hath God Wrought,' which was written by Anne Ellsworth, daughter of the Commissioner of Patents, was sent over the line by Morse. The next day, a telegram was

sent from Washington to the Baltimore 'Patriot.' In two years, telegraph lines linked Washington with Jersey City, and by 1849, the frail but influential wire strands stretched westward as far as Cincinnati. By 1857, Cincinnati had become the center of a network of 25,000 miles of telegraph lines.

The telegraph was recognized at once as a valuable means of communication for railroad operations, and soon a Telegraph Department was organized within the B&O system. By 1857, there were 30 telegraph stations between Baltimore and Wheeling. These stations reported on train movements and control operations.

Meanwhile, on 29 April 1851, another product of the inventive 1840s operated over the Washington Branch of the Baltimore & Ohio. This was the first *electric locomotive* for a standard railroad. Designed by Dr Charles Grafton Page of Salem, Massachusetts, this locomotive drew its power from heavy storage batteries. Modern electric locomotives usually draw power from an overhead wire or an electrified third rail.

Growth and Income and More Growth

More than $15.6 million was spent to complete the B&O to the Ohio River—three times the original estimate. Yet this sum was only the cost of the main line alone. With the Washington Branch and the Northwestern Virginia Railroad, plus additional tunnels, double tracking, new stations and equipment, the total spent by 1857 was more than $31 million. As the rails neared Wheeling, enough new equipment was ordered to double the B&O's existing rolling stock, and even this proved inadequate. By the fall of 1857, the number of B&O locomotives was increased to 236, and other stock included 3668 freight cars. These 3904 units of rolling stock constituted the largest fleet of any railroad then in operation in the United States.

Thomas Swann resigned from the B&O Presidency in April of 1853, and William G Harrison took his place immediately. Freight revenues now began to pour in. By 1854 the company was earning $3.4 million a year. In 1857, with the income of the Washington Branch Railroad included, the total income exceeded $5 million. Passenger traffic also was increasing. By 1857, more than 38,000 people traveled between Baltimore and Wheeling.

By then, ideas concerning transcontinental rail transportation began to gain (rather skeptical) audience throughout the country. In the 1820s and 1830s, it had seemed sufficient simply to link the Atlantic seaboard with the great navigable rivers of the interior, particularly the Ohio and the Mississippi. Along these, flat-bottomed steamboats would move the freight and passengers beyond the reach of the railroads.

River transportation soon was beginning to seem too slow, and frequently was hindered by low water, floods and freeze-ups. The B&O's Master of Transportation commented in 1854:

'For many years, the western rivers formed the great avenues of travel as well as of trade . . . The projection of the different railroad enterprises between the East and West looked only to reaching the western waters at points accessible by steamers . . . At the time at which the Baltimore & Ohio Railroad was opened to the Ohio River,

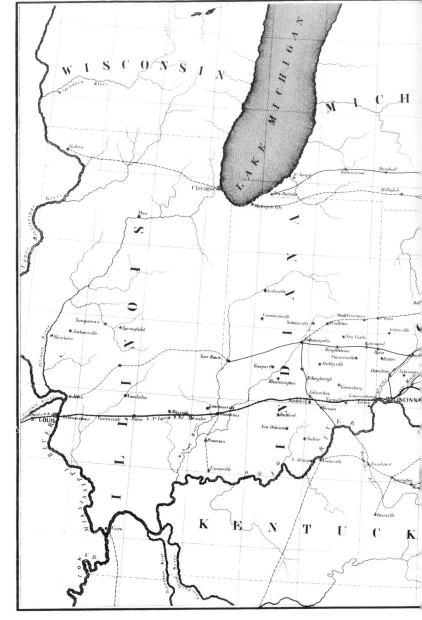

Previous page: An illustration of the frenzied way in which rail passengers took their meals in the pre-dining car era. *Below:* A drinking water kettle for passengers. *Above:* An 1843 railroad map.

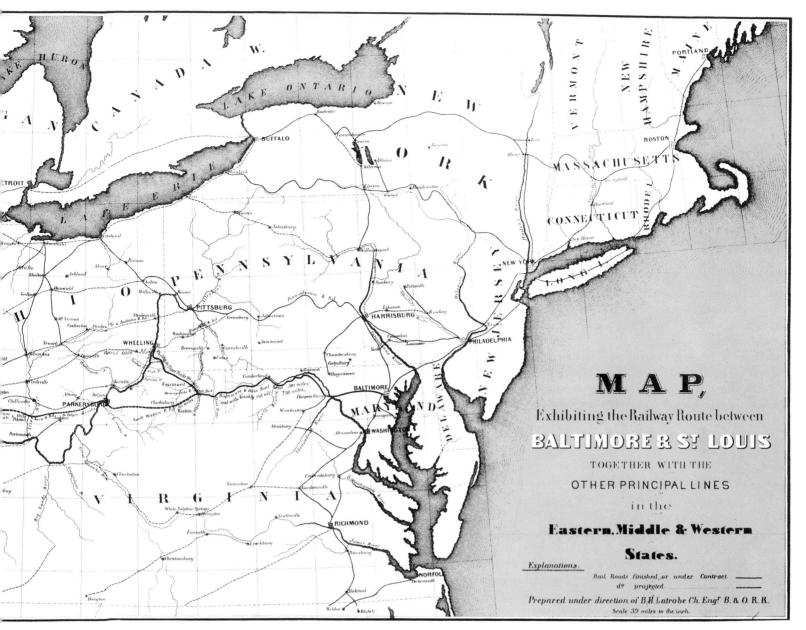

MAP,

Exhibiting the Railway Route between

BALTIMORE & St LOUIS

TOGETHER WITH THE

OTHER PRINCIPAL LINES

in the

Eastern, Middle & Western

States.

Explanations.

Rail Roads finished, or under Contract _____
d.º   projected ....

Prepared under direction of B.H. Latrobe Ch. Engr B.& O. R.R.
Scale 39 miles to the inch.

however, a change had commenced, and was going on with a rapidity which surprised all, even the most practical.

'The railroad lines leading from New York had formed continuous connections with Cincinnati and other important cities in the West, and the Pennsylvania Railroad enjoyed a similar advantage. The business travel, attracted by the great saving of time, had already been turned to these modern lines, leaving the great middle or national route over which for so many years it had continued to pass.' (The national route was the one via the National Road and the Ohio River.)

The Baltimore & Ohio set about the task of overcoming the advantages enjoyed by its competitor roads to the north. It had a valuable ally in the Central Ohio Railroad at Bellaire, Ohio—just across the river from Wheeling. There was a ferry system capable of moving all of the passengers and 1000 tons of freight per day between the two railroad terminals. The Central Ohio Railroad, incorporated in 1849 and opened as a through route in 1854, went on through Columbus, with connections there for Cincinnati. Thus, instead of exchanging the bulk of its traffic at Wheeling with the river boats, the B&O began to exchange freight and passengers with the Central Ohio and other new railroads of the West.

But even before Wheeling had been reached, the B&O Directors had turned to an even greater plan for westward expansion. Wheeling, it long had been realized, was not the most desirable western terminus. The city of Cincinnati, farther along the Ohio River, had grown and was still growing; it was a great midwestern trade center. Still farther west, St Louis was becoming an important Mississippi River terminus, and Wheeling was not on a direct line between Baltimore and these points.

For many years, Cincinnati had been a rich shipping center on the Ohio. But with the development of the northern US railroads, Cincinnati saw herself being bypassed by the trade, with the possibility of being left completely high and dry as Chicago began to flourish. This prompted Cincinnatians to take an active part in the initiation of railroad lines that would connect their city with the Atlantic seacoast to the east and with the Mississippi to the west. The Marietta & Cincinnati Railroad thus was founded to link Cincinnati with the Ohio River, and the Ohio & Mississippi was formed to link Cincinnati with the Mississippi at East St Louis.

In 1851, the Northwestern Virginia Railroad was incorporated under the sponsorship of the Baltimore & Ohio, which eventually absorbed it. The purpose of the Northwestern Virginia was to build a line west from Grafton, where the B&O's original main line turned north to Wheeling. This new line would end at Parkersburg; and across the Ohio River from Parkersburg was to be the eastern terminus of the Marietta & Cincinnati Railroad, already under construction.

Engineers and workmen threw their accumulated skill into the task of completing the new Parkersburg line. The Baltimore & Ohio subscribed $1.5 million toward the $5.4 million overall cost of the 103 mile road. Construction began in 1852, and the Northwestern Virginia was opened on 1 May 1857.

During this time, the scepter of the B&O Presidency passed from William Harrison to Chauncy Brooks on 14 November 1855. Brooks, like the several immediately preceding Presidents (and unlike the 12 year tenure of Louis McLane), would serve for just a few years.

The 'American Central Line'

The Marietta & Cincinnati and the Ohio & Mississippi also were put into service. The transfer across the Ohio between Parkersburg and Marietta was made by steamboat. The combination of these three roads constituted a route between St Louis and the East Coast that was 52 miles shorter than any other. With their completion, the 'American Central Line,' as the combined trackage of these roads was called, in fact did provide a trade corridor across the beltline of the eastern half of the US. The celebration that marked its opening outshone the lavishness of all previous railroad celebrations.

The grand feature of the affair was a railway excursion for hundreds of guests from the East Coast all the way through to St Louis (this was paralleled a month later by a similar excursion from the West to the East). The Baltimore & Ohio, the Marietta & Cincinnati and the Ohio & Mississippi each invited excursion parties. The aged Philip E Thomas, first President of the Baltimore & Ohio, was still alive to see the climax of his dream, but was unable to join the excursion because of illness.

The Baltimore & Ohio guests left Baltimore via special train, on the morning of 1 June 1857. As the excursion approached Cincinnati on 3 June, the passenger load had swelled to 2500 persons, many of them uninvited, and filled several trains. Thomas Swann, who was a member of the party despite his resignation from the B&O Presidency, predicted to the waiting crowd at Cincinnati:

'I congratulate you on what has been accomplished and upon those still more glorious results which are certain to be proclaimed when at no distant day the steel whistle sounding along the line of this great national highway shall be lost amidst the distant roar of the Pacific.'

Other trains chugged in from St Louis, with additional thousands of visitors. It was estimated that there were 20,000 visitors in Cincinnati for the celebration. That afternoon, there was interminable oratory and a fire fighting display during which a group of volunteer firemen, losing control of their hose, succeeded in attracting attention by knocking off the governor's hat. In the evening there was a grand ball.

On Thursday 4 June, the overburdened Ohio & Mississippi began shuttling the crowds out of Cincinnati and into St Louis for a celebration there on 5 and 6 June. The passengers detrained at Illinois Town, opposite St

Louis, and a fleet of excursion steamers transported them across the Mississippi. Friday and Saturday were spent with parades, pageantry, speeches and banquets, and the tired excursionists began straggling homeward on Sunday.

A second tour took place in July from the western cities into Baltimore, where the program included a mammoth banquet, a trip to Washington to meet President James Buchanan, and a boat trip down Chesapeake Bay.

The Late 1850s and John Garrett

Now, in 1857, the United States had 'grown up,' and the B&O had grown with it. The nation's first railroad now consisted of 519 miles of line, including the Washington, Locust Point and Frederick Branches, and the Northwestern Virginia Railroad. There were 226 miles of second track, additional sidings and other branch lines. The B&O also operated the Winchester & Potomac Railway and other tributary lines with an additional 77 miles of track. Along the B&O there were 85 freight and passenger stations, and in 1857 the road hauled nearly 203 million ton-miles of freight. At that point in time, there were nearly 5000 B&O employees.

At left: A view of an oil lamp inside a Civil War-era B&O passenger coach. *Below:* The *William Mason*, in a seeming face-off with a diesel from *this* century, in the B&O Museum in Baltimore.

There were many railroads in operation in America now. Four other railroads besides the B&O knifed through the Appalachian range from the Atlantic Coast. From Maine in the North, to North Carolina in the South, and from New York, Philadelphia and Baltimore in the East to Chicago and St Louis in the West, the bright lines of rails bound the nation together. There were almost enough miles of rail in the US to circle the earth.

The resulting growth of trade between the Northeast and the West enlarged and increased — by many fold — the cities and industries of New England and in the Middle Atlantic states. New York's population was in the vicinity of one million; and Baltimore's was two and one-half times what it had been in 1827, when the B&O was founded.

The increased wealth came primarily to the industrial North. The predominately agricultural South was dropping behind: the tension between South and North was increasing, and the drums of the American Civil War were beginning to beat in the background.

Into this uncomfortable milieu stepped John W Garrett, who took the reins of the B&O Presidency from Chauncy Brooks on 17 November 1858, and would hold that difficult office with great distinction until his death in 1884. Garrett's more than 25 years as the B&O's President would be exceeded only by the 31 year tenure of Daniel Willard in the following century.

THE CIVIL WAR YEARS

Seeds of Conflict

Slavery was outlawed in many parts of the world long before the American Civil War. The flames of violence in the United States were fanned by many years of internal disturbances and antagonisms, and were fed by bitter words from the pro-slavery faction and the abolitionists alike. Arguments had raged long and hard among statesmen and politicians concerning the issue of 'slave' or 'free' states.

The emotional conflict suddenly and terribly became a physical one. Bitter-hearted abolitionist John Brown had killed five men over the the slavery issue in his home town of Ossawatomie, Kansas, and had lost his son in the armed struggle. Brown fled from Kansas to Iowa and finally turned east toward Virginia, hiding out in the peaceful vicinity of Harper's Ferry.

Slowly, steadily, quietly, he collected arms and men to carry out his plans of freeing the slaves in an armed uprising. Unassuming and unnoticed, he prepared; and then, on 17 October 1859, his band of men rode into the town of Harper's Ferry, captured the government arsenal there, and threw a cordon of riflemen across the B&O tracks that passed through the arsenal grounds.

The eastbound night passenger express slowed to its scheduled stop at Harper's Ferry a few minutes later. Conductor AJ Phelps and Engineer William McKay found their train surrounded by armed men. Jacob Cromwell, the train's Baggage Master, stepped down with his lantern to find out what was wrong. In the darkness a shot was fired, and Station Porter Hayward Sheppard fell, dying. Other shots volleyed out. In the wild firing, Station Master Fontaine Beckham also was killed. A freight train crewman was injured when he and his fellows joined in the fight to help their fellow railroaders.

More angry than frightened, Phelps ordered the train backed away from the violence, and personally sought out the leader of the armed band. He demanded that the train be allowed to proceed. Brown gave this permission, but neglected to order away the men who blocked the track. Phelps therefore decided to 'stand pat' until daylight. The train got under way at the crack of dawn, and at Monocacy, Conductor Phelps wired Baltimore. His hastily scribbled description of the uprising mistakenly named the leader as 'Anderson' and estimated the number of the band at 150.

At first, WP Smith, the Master of Transportation at Baltimore, was inclined to consider the incident a minor one. He replied by wire, accusing Phelps of exaggeration. Indignantly, Phelps answered:

'My dispatch was not exaggerated, neither was it written under excitement, as you suppose. I have not made it half as bad as it is. The captain told me that his object was to liberate all the slaves and that he expected a reinforcement of 1500 men to assist him. Hayward, the Negro Porter, was shot through the body, and I suppose by this time is dead. The captain also said that he did not want to shed any more blood.

'I will call at your office immediately on my arrival and tell you all. One of my passengers was taken prisoner and held as such for some time. I will bring him to see you also.'

Belatedly, Smith leaped to action. He reached B&O President Garrett, who notified the Secretary of War,

The B&O was vital to the Union Civil War effort, and was ever in the thick of the action. *Previous page:* A photograph of the B&O Shops at Martinsburg, West Virginia in the early 1860s. Shown here are Camelback locomotives and a train composed of the then-common 'iron pot' coal cars. The large polygonal engine house in the background, and most of the other buildings in this compound, suffered destruction by Confederate forces in October of 1862. Equipment all along the B&O lines was wrecked repeatedly by both sides as the tide of war swept back and forth over the area. *At right:* Harper's Ferry, Virginia, before the Civil War, when West Virginia was still part of Virginia. It was here that John Brown and his raiders struck in October of 1859 (see the text, this page). Note the single convered bridge crossing the Potomac. In the photo *below* — of Harper's Ferry, *West* Virginia, in the 1940s — we see the piers of the now-dismantled covered bridge to the left. Two modern steel bridges have replaced the old span across the river, and there is evidence of added rail trackage.

At left: Abraham Lincoln arrives in the nation's capital for his first term as President on 23 February 1861. The B&O train on which he arrived is in the background. *Above:* A restored 'iron pot' hopper car of the Civil War era, in the B&O Railroad Museum.

John B Floyd. To quell the uprising, Floyd sent a detachment of 90 Marines under Colonel Robert E Lee, who later was to command the Confederate Army. The abolitionist leader and his followers were captured after a pitched battle, and Brown was tried and hanged less than two months later, on 2 December 1859.

This was the introduction to the coming conflict for the Baltimore & Ohio. Through the war years, the relationship between the railroad and the US government grew ever more close. Garrett, who at first had felt sympathy for the South, grew to become a loyal supporter of the North and a fast friend of President Lincoln.

A Vital Artery

Among Marylanders, there was much difference of opinion, although at first most of them were strongly pro-Southern in attitude and sympathy. That Maryland did not join the seceding Southern states—and that Washington, the Union capital in the very midst of the fighting theater, was saved from what would have been a very great threat indeed—was in large part due to the influence of the Baltimore & Ohio.

The railroad linked Maryland and northwestern Virginia to the North by economic and political bands that were too strong to be broken, and it provided strong security for the city of Washington, as it was the main corridor of access for reinforcing Union troops from the North and West coming into the District of Columbia area.

And, because the Baltimore & Ohio was the main east-west route for Union troop transport for operations along the wide front from the Atlantic seaboard to the Mississippi River, the railroad was a crucial military freight and troop transport for the Union war effort in general.

After John Brown's raid, events leading to war had crowded fast one upon the other. Abraham Lincoln, leader of the newly-formed Republican Party, made his famous speech against slavery at Cooper Union, and was voted into the Presidency in 1860. South Carolina seceded from the Union in December of that same year. In February of 1861, Lincoln set out from Springfield to take up his new duties in Washington, and South Carolina organized the Confederacy.

Jefferson Davis was elected President of the Confederacy on 8 February. In his inaugural address on 4 March 1861, Lincoln denied the right of the Confederate States to secede. The Confederate answer to Lincoln's veto was the shelling of Fort Sumter in Charleston Harbor on 12 April of that year. They captured the fort two days later. Lincoln called up 75,000 militiamen, and asked also for 65,000 volunteers. War had come, and both sides had armies in the field.

A Railroad at War

On 18 and 19 April, Northern soldiers were passing through Baltimore to Washington. Mobs of Southern sympathizers tore up the B&O tracks along Pratt Street to prevent passage of the railroad cars carrying the troops. (In those days, the railroad still was prohibited from operating engines along the streets of downtown Baltimore. Passenger cars transferring from the Philadelphia, Wilmington & Baltimore to the B&O had to be pulled by horse over the connecting tracks through the center of the city.)

At the same time, Union troops destroyed the Harper's Ferry Arsenal and withdrew in the face the Virginia Militia. With this demolition and withdrawal, part of the B&O mainline fell into the hands of the Confederates, although B&O trains were still allowed to operate over it.

Except for brief interruptions caused by small clashes, trains operated between Baltimore, Wheeling and Parkersburg until 25 May, when a great overhanging rock near Point of Rocks, Maryland, was blasted from its hillside onto the track. The next day, two bridges at

Buffalo Creek, in what is now West Virginia, were burned out by Confederate forces.

Workmen cleared the rock and trestled the gaps within two days. By then, though, the Confederates held more than 100 miles of the main line between Point of Rocks and Cumberland. In June and July of 1861, Confederates ravaged Martinsburg and damaged the machine shops, the engine houses and other railroad buildings, in addition to confiscating 14 locomotives. These they hauled back down South, using teams of horses to pull the engines along the old dirt roads of the time, since sufficient fuel and trackage to the South was not quite yet available.

Other battles, sweeping over the right-of-way, resulted in the burning of 42 other locomotives and at least 386 cars between May and October of 1861. Twenty-three bridges were destroyed in that time; 36 and one-half miles of track and more than 100 miles of telegraph lines were torn down. Innumerable buildings were destroyed, and two additional locomotives were driven into the Potomac River. In the fall, General Stonewall Jackson's raiding forces added to the destruction, tearing up 40

more miles of track and wrecking more bridges, buildings and other equipment. Floods swept out trestles over creeks and rivers between the Monocacy River in Maryland and the Ohio River at Wheeling.

As soon as the Confederate forces were thrown back, however, the railroad trackmen went to work rebuilding the line. Before the end of March 1862, the entire route was in service. But this happy situation lasted for barely two months. By 25 May 1862, General Bank's Union forces had to fall back from Winchester, and the Confederate Army again took possession of the B&O's line in Virginia.

The South Invades

In few areas did the tide of battle flow back and forth so often and so suddenly as it did in the Potomac Valley. The Union men recovered the western portion of the B&O

At left: An illustration of the Union's Seventh Regiment of New York, as it arrived at the B&O's Washington, DC, station in 1861. *Below:* A B&O iron boxcar typical of the kind that was used to transport gunpowder for the Union forces during the Civil War.

main line in the first half of June 1862, and service was renewed, only to be interrupted again three months later. General Lee, making his first invasion of Maryland (between Harper's Ferry and the Monocacy River) with 55,000 men, threw back the Union Army in early September 1862, in what was to become famous as the Antietam Campaign.

In two and one-half months, Lee's forces destroyed 35 miles of the mainline west of Harper's Ferry, tore down 90 miles of telegraph lines, burned the bridge over the Little Cacapon River and damaged many other railroad structures.

Lee's Confederate forces wrought more destruction upon the important railroad center of Martinsburg than it suffered at any other time during the war. The large, polygonal engine house and the smaller semi-circular engine shop were burned, along with the machine shops, the company's hotel, a warehouse, the ticket and telegraph offices, the master mechanic's house, the coal storage bins, the blacksmith shop, the pump and water stations and miles of telegraph lines.

This great destruction at Martinsburg occurred on 19 and 20 October 1862. In destroying the track, the Confederate soldiers made great bonfires of the ties, and upon this fire they laid the steel rails. The rails became hot and pliable, and these iron ribbons were then twisted around tree trunks so they could not be used again. This was a practice also used by the North, under the direction of the US War Department's General Herman Haupt, a railroad construction-engineering genius. In fact, the North may well have invented this practice which made for many an uncanny landscape. Rails so wrapped around trees were known as 'Union bow ties.' Altogether, the destruction wrought by both sides on the nation's railroads was phenomenal—due in large part to such inventiveness.

Apart from the violence of the war proper, the railroad was plagued during lulls in the fighting by the individual

Civil War construction and destruction. At left: A Union work party modifies a right of way. Note that the locomotive is named for the Union engineer, General Herman Haupt. *Below:* Confederates sabotage trackage. *At right:* Union raiders tear up track and make 'Union bow ties' by wrapping heated rails around trees. *Below right:* A temporary construction to replace a demolished bridge.

soldiers of both armies who removed cattle sheds, tool houses, and other railroad buildings to construct winter quarters. In the miscellany of calamity, one finds mention of a huge fire at Camden Station, Baltimore, in September of 1862, and the theft of the great locomotive turntable at Martinsburg by the Confederates. Scores of other mishaps added to the chaos, in the midst of which the railroad tried to maintain service.

By December of 1862, the Union forces had regained possession of the B&O in western Virginia, which was soon to become the 'state of West Virginia,' and the entire line again was restored to service on 6 January 1863. But in April 1863, the Confederate Generals William E Jones and John D Imboden swept north over the B&O

into western Maryland and western Virginia. The purposes of their raids, carried out with 5800 men, were several: to capture the Union forces in western Virginia; to overthrow the Union-loyal Virginia government at Wheeling; to recruit Confederate sympathizers in the area; to secure livestock, horses and supplies; and to cut the Baltimore & Ohio Railroad at as many points as possible, so that it could not be used by the Union Army.

During the Jones-Imboden raids, one troop captured a loaded B&O stock train at Altamont and forced the engineer to run it into Confederate territory. Other raiders displaced the approaches to the Youghiogheny Bridge, causing a locomotive to crash into the river. Subsequently, the same bridge was totally destroyed, along with the water station at Altamont, Maryland, and the water station and engine house at Cranberry Summit (now Terra Alta, West Virginia). The track at Altamont also was torn up.

The Union guards on the Cheat River Bridge were attacked on the night of 26 April, but they repulsed the Confederate forces. Next day the raiders fell upon nearby Newburg, in western Virginia, burned many railroad buildings, destroyed 300 feet of track, and blew up an iron bridge. On the 28th, they moved on to Kingwood and Morgantown, and thence to Fairmont. At the Monon-

gahela River near Fairmont, they captured the Union guard, and not without difficulty—for the Confederate engineers had to detonate three separate charges to blow up the bridge there, which was the largest iron bridge on the road at that time.

Continuing the orgy of destruction, the Confederate soldiers burned additional bridges at Coal Run, Buffalo Creek, Finche's Run, Cappo Fork and Church's Fork, and destroyed miles of roadbed and telegraph lines at other points.

As before, immediately behind the raiders moved the railroad reconstruction parties. By 2 May, telegraph service was fully restored, and two days later, the entire road was opened from Baltimore to Wheeling—except for the Monongahela Bridge, where the gap was bridged temporarily by pontoons. Within 10 days, the Monongahela was re-trestled. Trains were making uninterrupted runs by 17 May—barely more than a week after the tide of 'raiders in gray' had begun their retreat Southward, feeling (mistakenly) confident that the destruction they had wrought could not be quickly undone.

Upon his return, General Jones reported to General Lee that his men had destroyed two trains, 16 rail bridges and one railroad tunnel, had captured 700 Union soldiers and had seized 1000 cattle and 1200 horses.

And all this despite the efforts of a Union guard of 10,000 men along the main line from Harper's Ferry to the Ohio River, and 15,000 additional Union troops in the vicinity. Even so, the quick-reactive ingenuity of the B&O crews and the Union workparties in restoring the road certainly ameliorated the raid's success.

The South Tries Again

The South began its second great invasion of Maryland and points north in June, 1863. It was his most serious threat against the North, and on June 3, the Northern border was agog with rumors of an advance by mighty forces under General Lee. Operation of trains west of Monocacy was limited to the night hours when darkness offered a degree of safety. Two days later, there were reports that the Confederates were crossing the Potomac at Point of Rocks, Maryland, but despite this, the Baltimore & Ohio trains continued to move through.

The Confederate troops that had been sighted at Point of Rocks were actually light reconnaissance forces. A Northward movement by a strong advance guard began in Virginia on 13 June, and the master of transportation for the B&O arranged to have all engines, cars and other rolling stock moved to the East from Martinsburg. The main body of Union forces, falling back from Winchester, moved through Martinsburg on 14 June and on to Williamsport; there was heavy rear guard fighting in Martinsburg. By eight pm, the telegraph lines to the west of Harper's Ferry had been cut. The west-bound B&O mail train that night went only as far as Sandy Hook, opposite Harper's Ferry on the east bank of the Potomac.

A large group of Confederates crossed the Potomac at Point of Rocks on 17 June. They captured a B&O train of 17 cars and destroyed it. The troops moved Northward still. Harper's Ferry fell. Meanwhile, the wreckage at Point of Rocks was cleared by railroad workers so that the rolling stock at Sandy Hook could be moved farther

At far left: Engineers of the US Military Railroad Construction Corps with their tools and surveying instruments in 1864. War-damaged locomotives were often transported back to the shops for refurbishing, as is shown *above. Below:* A hasty bridge repair.

east to safety in Baltimore.

At the beginning of the campaign, Lee's forces overwhelmed everything in their path and gained possession of 160 miles of main line. They were in control at intervals from Sykesville, only 30 miles west of Baltimore, to the ridges of the Alleghenies. In this area, they destroyed 27 miles of track and 92 miles of telegraph lines, much of the rolling stock and other equipment.

Every major bridge between Cumberland and Harper's Ferry was destroyed. Despite the complete disruption of through service, an attempt was made to operate trains in the West, from Cumberland to the western terminals at Wheeling and Parkersburg.

The great battle at Gettysburg, Pennsylvania took place from the first to the third of July, and on these hot summer days, Lee went down in resounding, bloody defeat before Meade's Northern forces. After Gettysburg, the Confederates fell back into Virginia, and construction crews immediately went to work to repair the railroad west of Harper's Ferry.

The workmen of the reconstruction crews were protected by an iron-clad train that was protected by a military guard. Another new feature in railroading during the year 1863 was the prefabrication of iron bridges at the B&O's Mount Clare shops in Baltimore. These structures were tailor made to replace the trestles at Monocacy, Harper's Ferry, Martinsburg and other points where such had been destroyed.

Before the weary survivors of what had been Lee's force of 75,000 men had straggled back to the Southland from the debacle at Gettysburg, Master of Transportation WP Smith had the B&O line back in operation all the way from Baltimore to Wheeling and Parkersburg. By 11 August, trains were in operation on all B&O and affiliated routes.

Trains to the Rescue

A little later, there occurred the greatest mass movement of troops by rail up to that time. The B&O played an important part in this movement, which was initiated on 23 September 1863, when Secretary of War Edwin Stanton received word of the defeat and retreat of General William S Rosecrans at the battle of Chickamauga, in Georgia. Rosecrans asked for reinforcements. The natural gateway through which reinforcements could be sent to him was Nashville, Tennessee.

President Garrett of the B&O, Lincoln's principal advisor on transportation; General George G Meade, Commander of the Army of the Potomac; General Henry W Halleck, Military Advisor to the President, and TT Eckert, head of the Army's telegraph communications, immediately were called into conference. Later, President Lincoln himself joined the meeting which lasted all night.

It was decided to send part of the Army of the Potomac to Rosecrans' assistance. But the problem of moving approximately 20,000 men, with their horses, mules, baggage and heavy guns from the Potomac Valley to Georgia, all in a few days, seemed impossible.

At first Eckert, who later became President of the Western Union Telegraph Company, estimated that the movement would require 50 to 60 days. But after additional study of railroad timetables, Eckert predicted it could be made in 15 days. This seemed incredible to the others.

The route Eckert decided upon was a circuitous one, northeastward from Washington over the B&O to Benwood in what had by then become West Virginia.

At right: This 1860 map shows the major eastern rail lines at the time of the Civil War. The B&O's access to the US capital, and its southern location, made it crucial to the Union war effort.

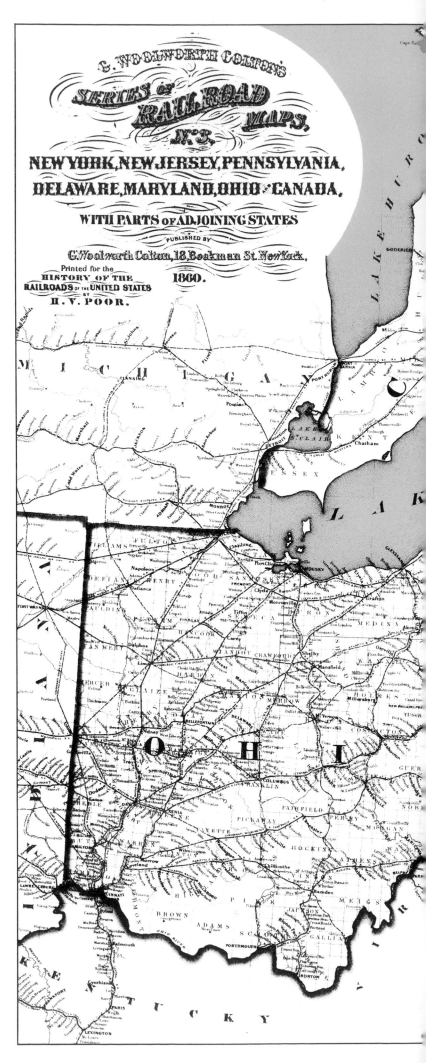

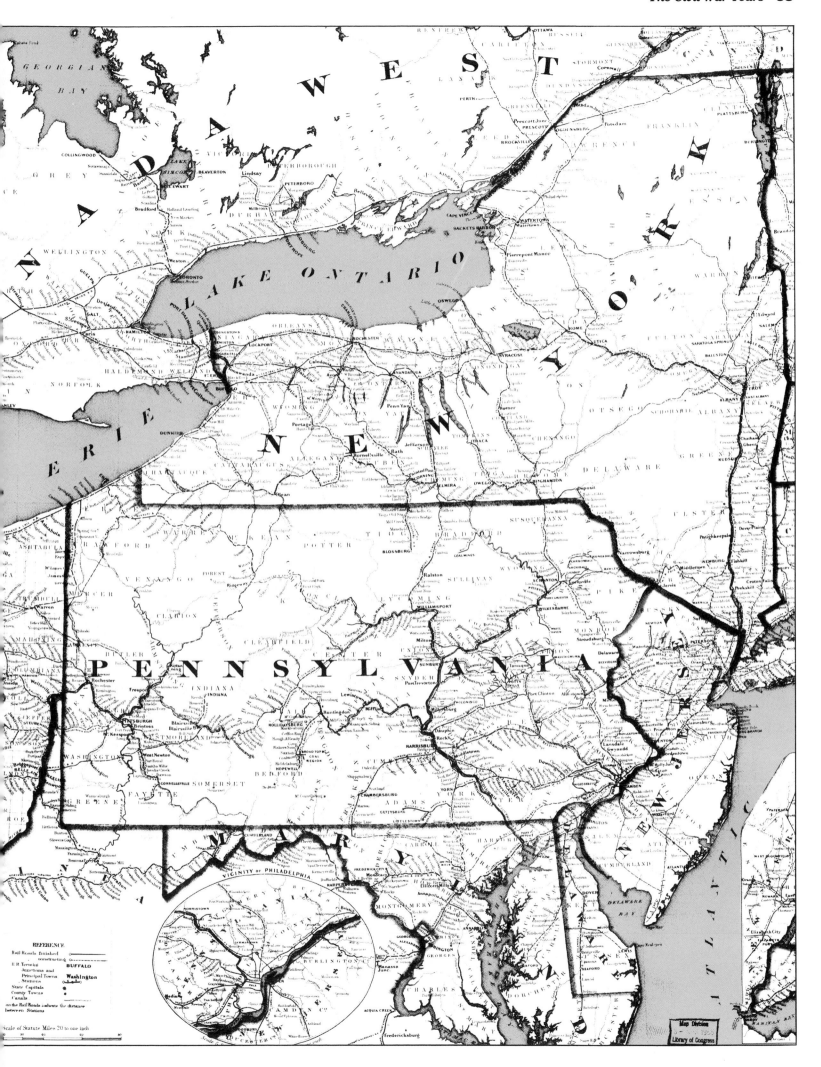

There, the troops would move across the Ohio River on a pontoon bridge to entrain again at Bellaire, Ohio, for an uninterrupted movement to Indianapolis, thence south to Louisville, southwest to Nashville, and finally southeast to Bridgeport in the northeastern corner of Alabama, just across the Georgia border.

'Fightin' Joe' Hooker, in command of the Army of the Potomac's 11th and 12th Corps, said that it couldn't be done. Despite his objections, Stanton arranged to carry out the plan. Eckert was assigned to work with the Quartermaster Corps on a plan to establish relays of cooks, waiters, food and cooking equipment so that food could be served to the men on the trains as their cars passed the established feeding points along the route.

John W Garrett and WP Smith worked out the operational details with representatives of the other railroads involved. The railroad men assembled all available cars, regardless of type—box cars, freight cars, passenger cars, work cars—and on the morning of 25 September, the first troops assembled in Washington to entrain.

When the first trainload arrived at Benwood, West Virginia, the pontoon bridge was ready, and the Central Ohio Railroad had trains waiting across the river at Bellaire. At Columbus, Ohio, the men were transferred to the Indiana Central Railroad, which carried them on to Indianapolis. There the Jeffersonville, Madison & Indianapolis narrow gauge road took over. The Ohio

River between Jeffersonville and Louisville had been bridged with coal barges, and by four am on 29 September, the vanguard of the force was passing over this makeshift bridge. New trainloads were arriving in Louisville, Kentucky, at three hour intervals. From Louisville they moved south, and within 11 days after the movement had begun, some 20,000 men, 100 carloads of equipment, 10 batteries of field guns and hundreds of mules and horses had arrived at the scene of action. Eckert's estimate had been wrong—he had thought this massive movement would take four days longer.

The End Nears

The year 1864 was marked by only one prolonged interruption of the B&O main line, yet there were constant short interruptions and difficulties as the heavy campaigning moved Southward and the Northern front lapsed into spasmodic fighting. Raiding parties, ambushes, guerrilla forces *and* floods combined to wreak new havoc.

In this year of the South's dying cause, the most serious incident occurred in the summer as the result of Lieutenant General Jubal Early's invasion along the Shenandoah Valley, the last Confederate venture-in-force north of the Potomac. Early's raid began on 2 July, and not until 19 September was his blockade of the line lifted, following General Sheridan's Union victory at Winchester, Virginia. By 27 September, trains again were operating over the rebuilt tracks and bridges throughout the valley of the Potomac.

The year 1864 was noteworthy for another event, which was not directly connected with the war: the first steel rails to be used by a railroad in America were put in use on the B&O. The last year of the war, 1865, saw some of the heaviest troop movements of the Civil War period.

The War is Over

A great moment was the departure from the Washington area of the combined Union forces of Grant and Sherman. These armed forces had come to the capital for a victory review after General Lee — representing the Confederacy — surrendered at Appomattox Court House in Virginia, on 9 April 1865.

Thus, in July 1865, 233,000 troops were moved out of the B&O passenger station in Washington. Of these, 96,000 traveled over the full length of the B&O main line

Harper's Ferry, site of a US Armory, suffered major Confederate raids in 1861 and 1863. *At left:* The B&O Depot there — seven decades later, in 1931. *Below:* A view of the bridges leading out of town, in 1981 — by then, the B&O had also served the US in two world wars and had become part of CSX Corporation (see page 127).

to Parkersburg, whence 92 steamers carried them on to Cincinnati, Louisville and other down-river cities. The war was over, but the railroad's war-born liabilities were still in evidence. Flooded rivers crashed down from the Alleghenies, destroying everything in their paths. Also, even after the formal surrender, Confederate-sympathetic guerrilla forces continued to interfere with railroad operations.

So it was that, both during and after both armies had wreaked their full vengeance upon the B&O, the railroad's right-of-way was also battered by floods and weather of unusual violence. Raging waters thundered down the Potomac and Ohio and their tributaries again and again, repeatedly washed out many of the strongest bridges, sweeping away rolling stock, wrecking telegraph lines and other installations.

The B&O's record of war- and weather-related disaster from 1861 to 1865 is one of monotonous destruction unequaled in the annals of private industry in America. Hundreds of thousands of dollars were spent to put the line into service after each calamity. That the railroad's engineers and workers — in conjunction with the US War Department's brilliant construction engineer General Herman Haupt and his men — rebuilt the road so quickly again and again, in the face of enemy gunfire and terribly destructive storms, is a tribute to their resiliency, skill and courage.

EXPANSION AND A TROUBLED ECONOMY

Assassination, Progress and Economic Woes

The South had surrendered and the fighting was done, but the land was not peaceful. Shortly after Appomattox, the actor John Wilkes Booth assassinated President Lincoln, who was just entering his second term as President. In the land of chaos that had been the Confederacy, the Ku Klux Klan sprang to life, fostering new violence and hatred. Lincoln's Vice President, Andrew Johnson, succeeded to the Presidency. President Johnson had the unfortunate distinction of being the first US President to be impeached by the Senate, and was acquitted by a single vote. In the bitter politics of the time, no one was spared; even Lincoln's widow was slandered openly in Congress.

On 24 September 1869, aka 'Black Friday,' the US economy crashed. But with all the confusion, there was still advancement. The first transcontinental telegraph line had been completed in 1862, and the first transatlantic telegraph line was completed in 1866. The United States purchased Alaska and its vast store of natural resources from Russia for $7.2 million in 1867. The first transcontinental rail route in America was completed on 10 May 1869, when the golden spike was driven into the connecting tie at Promontory, Utah, to join the Central Pacific and Union Pacific Railroads. That same year, George Westinghouse patented his air brake, which was to play such an important part in railroad safety progress. George Pullman built his first sleeping cars, diners and parlor cars, to provide rail passengers of that decade with previously unheard-of amenities.

The B&O decided to double-track its main stem through to Cumberland. The Washington Branch line of the B&O already had been double-tracked during the war years, when its importance in the protection of the nation's capital had become apparent.

The after effects of the Civil War were to be reflected by the Baltimore & Ohio for many years. The $2 million income of 1852 had seemed enormous at the time, but with the end of the war total income topped $10 million a year. The war had actually helped to *strengthen* the road economically and administratively. Physically, of course, the B&O was in terrible shape, and a difficult job of reconstruction lay ahead—for the postwar years saw revenues falling off from the phenomenal figure just cited, and the B&O's trackage had to be rebuilt, improved and extended, and the rolling stock had to be upgraded and modernized.

Garrett Leads the Way

It was a busy decade for the B&O. New projects were initiated by the score. The double tracking of the main stem went forward under the leadership of B&O President John W Garrett, whose plans for expansion exceeded the greatest dreams of the B&O's founders. Garrett foresaw mighty rivals in the New York Central, the Pennsylvania and the Erie railroads of the North

Previous page: The B&O's 4-6-0 *Thatcher Perkins*, built for 1860s passenger service, on exhibit at the Fair of the Iron Horse (see page 89). *At right:* The exterior of a Pullman sleeper car. *Above far right:* A sleeper with pull-down upper—*and* convertible lower—berths. *Above right:* A Pullman lounge/sleeper car of the 1870s.

—for those lines reached westward into the same general area as the B&O and could easily carry off the bulk of the western trade.

President Garrett set about increasing his control of the Marietta & Cincinnati Railroad, thus to insure improvement of the B&O's link with St Louis, on the trade-heavy Mississippi. His next task was to repair the weakest links in the B&O's main line. These were at the Ohio River area gaps, where B&O trains still had to be ferried across the river at Parkersburg and Wheeling. Railroad bridges were necessary if efficient service was to be provided. The Wheeling bridge was begun in 1868, and was finished within 37 months. A gigantic structure, its length, including approaches, was 8566 feet. At Parkersburg, the second huge bridge was begun in 1869, and opened in January of 1871.

Together, these bridges cost more than $2.3 million, but they soon proved their worth.

Garrett hoped to extend the B&O's northern main line as far west as Chicago. Chicago was showing ample evidence of its national importance, and this growing commercial giant was already linked to the East Coast by another railroad. Not only did Garrett wish to reach Chicago, he also wished to connect with the other major ports along the Great Lakes—Detroit, Cleveland and perhaps, even Buffalo.

This ambition began bearing fruit in 1869, when the B&O bought the Central Ohio Railroad. This line carried the B&O into Sandusky, Ohio, which was one of the best harbors on Lake Erie, and gave the B&O a continuous line of 595 miles from Baltimore to Sandusky: the distance to Chicago thus was more than half bridged.

In the 1870s, B&O President Garrett concentrated his attention on completing the line to Chicago. He struck out westward from the Sandusky line directly toward Chicago, a distance of 275 miles. The junction with the Sandusky road first was called Chicago Junction (it was later renamed 'Willard Junction,' in honor of the B&O's great twentieth century President, Daniel Willard. The line from Baltimore to Chicago was 811 miles long—and the line from Washington to Chicago (a most lucrative stretch of track) was 784 miles. It went into operation in November of 1874.

In 1891, the B&O achieved a shorter route to Chicago by the acquisition of the Pittsburgh & Western Railroad; the Pittsburgh, Cleveland & Toledo Railroad; and the Akron & Chicago Junction Railroad.

There long had been agitation for a shorter line to connect Washington with Point of Rocks, Maryland, thus providing a more direct route from the nation's capital to the West. The existing trackage required that Washington's westbound trains run east as far as Relay, Maryland, before turning onto the main stem. The new short line between Washington and Point of Rocks, which came to be called the 'Metropolitan Branch,' was completed in 1868. The old main line was, however, maintained for years as a route by which freight trains by-passed the urban congestion of Washington.

New Venues, New Horizons

A man of extraordinary vision, John W Garrett saw that any increase in the freight tonnage carried by the B&O between Baltimore and the West would depend to a large extent upon the development of greater port facilities in Baltimore Harbor, so as to expand Baltimore's import and export trade, and thus increase the flow of goods. Therefore, Garrett turned his intentions to the building of a railroad-owned dock area, so that freight trains could be brought onto the docks and freight could be transferred between ship and rail car without intermediate handling.

Garrett's vision produced one of the greatest railroad marine terminals in the world. It became known as the B&O Marine Terminal, with an efficient complex of warehouses, grain elevators, special handling facilities, yards, slips and wharves for accommodating the global freight market.

Garrett also established his own steamship line. It started with a fleet of three freighters that had been built by the government for wartime use: these were purchased by the B&O when the Civil War ended. For three years, these ships operated across the Atlantic, and

Below: Artwork of an 1875 Mogul type locomotive, built at the Mount Clare Shops for B&O passenger service on steep grades. *At right:* The B&O Marine Terminal in Baltimore (see text, this page).

Such nineteenth century B&O rolling stock as 2-6-0 Mogul type passenger locomotive Number 600 *JC Davis* (*above*, on the left — and also see caption, page 60) and Number 545, a 2-8-0 Consolidation-type freight locomotive named *AJ Cromwell* (*above*, on the right), were state-of-the-art for their time. The above photo was taken in the Baltimore Railroad Museum in 1973.

although the line was never expanded, it served Garrett's purpose by helping to stimulate shipping to and from Baltimore. With the demise of its own steamship line, the B&O entered into an agreement, with the famous North German Lloyd Steamship Company, that would bring a lot of business to the facilities at Baltimore.

The United States celebrated its 100th birthday as a nation in 1876. It was both a good time and a bad time, but fortunately the good overshadowed the bad. This was the year of the Centennial Exposition in Philadelphia, which was the first world's fair to be held in the United States. It was also the year of Alexander Graham Bell's first telephone; and — as if in example of the extremes to which the pendulum of fortune sometimes swings — of General George Armstrong Custer's annihilation at the Battle of the Little Big Horn.

As a matter of fact, the decade of 1870–80 saw the advent of the first typewriters, the first railroad refrigerator cars and the first tank cars for transporting oil and other liquids by rail. Colorado, the 38th State, had just been admitted to the Union, and the center of US population was moving westward. Ohio, Illinois and Missouri — the latter *beyond* the Mississippi, ranked 3rd, 4th and 5th, respectively — in the order of the size of their populations, in relation to all of the then-existing states — with only New York and Pennsylvania ahead of them to represent the eastern seaboard.

cutthroat competition that lasted for more than a decade. The railroads refused to cooperate with each other in establishing reasonable rates for freight and passengers, and as the depression reached its lowest ebb, the competing rates were cut so low that the roads could not hope to operate without loss. With the other roads, the Baltimore & Ohio was caught in the evil cycle. In those hectic days, greater business for the railroads meant only greater losses for their owners. Many railroads were 'forced to the wall,' and went bankrupt.

The situation began to clear after the railroads in the Northeast organized a 'Trunk Line Association' to make a survey and determine fair rates for freight hauled between interior cities and the seaports. The result of this agreement was to give Baltimore a slightly lower rate than was enjoyed by Philadelphia, New York and Boston, because Baltimore was closer to the interior than they were. The same agreement divided freight into six different major classes, with the rates varying according to class.

With the passing of the 1870s, better times arrived for the country as a whole, and for the railroads in particular. Passenger and freight earnings jumped quickly as business increased. In 1887, the Interstate Commerce Act was passed by Congress, and railroad rates and practices since that time have been increasingly under the control of the Interstate Commerce Commission. While a complete solution was not immediately forthcoming, the formation of the ICC, and the efforts of the Pennsylvania Railroad's AJ Cassatt to get more rates regulation enacted, did in fact pay off eventually.

Tracks to Philadelphia and Other Improvements

When the B&O began operating its own trains through to New York in the 1870s, it used the tracks of the Philadelphia, Wilmington & Baltimore Railroad as far as Philadelphia, and then Pennsylvania Railroad trackage from there into Jersey City. To eliminate its operations over the lines of the Pennsylvania, which was one of its chief competitors, the B&O later arranged to use the tracks of the Philadelphia & Reading and of the Jersey Central Railroads between Philadelphia and New York.

In 1881, the Philadelphia, Wilmington & Baltimore Railroad fell into the hands of a group of Boston financiers. Both the B&O and the Pennsylvania sought to buy the PW&B from them—the former to assure continuance of its trackage rights to Philadelphia, and the latter to prevent this. When the Pennsylvania won the battle by paying an above par price for each share, the B&O's John W Garrett immediately decided to *build* his own line to Philadelphia.

Until 1883, the B&O, like other railroads, operated its trains on schedules that were based on the local time at one or more of the principal cities along its line—this made for somewhat erratic coordination of schedules from one city to another. Therefore, on November 18 of that year, the B&O and more than 60 other railroads consorted to establish the now-familiar standard time system which would provide the United States with five different standard time zones, one hour apart. Informally adopted country-wide by communities, counties and states, this time system was made official in 1918.

Economic Woes, Rates Wars and Labor Troubles

Despite the ravages of the Indian Wars, the transcontinental railroads and the telegraph lines were making the Atlantic and Pacific coasts seem at last to be part of a united nation. However, in national, state and local governments, there was corruption, and in the field of business, there were years of depression; many businesses were forced into bankruptcy, and many workers were unemployed.

In the midst of the depression of 1877, the Baltimore & Ohio and the other American railroads suffered from a widespread and violent railroad strike that was precipitated by payroll cuts and new work practices. At the same time, most American railroads entered upon an era of

In October 1884 the PW&B, now under 'Pennsy' control, refused the B&O the privilege of using its tracks, but two years later, on 19 September 1886, B&O trains began operating to Philadelphia over the B&O's own newly constructed line.

Robert Garrett Takes Over

John Garrett's long tenure of more than 25 years as President of the B&O ended with his death in November 1884. His son, Robert, became acting President of the system which John Garrett had built into a powerful, efficient rail line that stretched from New York and Baltimore, in the East, to Chicago and St Louis, in the West.

The decade of the 1880s saw considerable improvements in the passenger service of the B&O, especially in

Above: A latter nineteenth century passenger coach, with reversible seatbacks for more versatile seating, and wide, pull down sleeping berths. *Above far right:* The legendary John W Garrett, B&O President from 1858–84, and whose tenure was exceeded only by that of Daniel Willard (see page 75). *At far right:* Charles F Mayer, who honorably served as B&O President from 1888–96.

regard to faster schedules. It was all started by an event connected with the Republican National Convention of 1884 in Chicago. The B&O had promised to bring a group of Washington newspaper men back from the convention to the nation's capital at top speed on a special train. The train made the distance of 784 miles in a record time of 22 and one-half hours, despite many handicaps. At one point, the train covered six miles in less than four minutes.

This was a remarkable record for the time, and it provided a suggestion to new B&O President Robert Garrett. If this speed could be made by one train, Garrett reasoned, all regular trains could likewise reduce their time. He had all passenger schedules speeded up accordingly.

A standardization that was of great value to the nation was achieved in 1886, after many years of effort. A standard railway track width, or gauge, was established and adopted by the vast majority of railroads in the US. Previous to this, some 23 different railway gauges had been in use. These ranged from two to six feet, and all were converted to the new standard of four feet eight and one-half inches — the gauge that had been used by the B&O from its beginning. This made possible the transfer and free interchange of freight and passenger cars throughout the nation.

Robert Garrett remained President only until 12 October 1887, when poor health prompted his resignation. Board of Directors member William Burns was elected *president pro tem*, and served until Samuel Spencer's election to the B&O Presidency on 10 December 1887. Due to disagreements with the Board of Directors, Spencer resigned his office a year later — in light of the difficulties that would soon overtake the B&O, it would probably have been wise of the B&O Board to have supported Spencer's views on cutting costs and establishing a sounder financial base for the railroad. He later became the first President of the Southern Railway and built it into one of the nation's great railroad systems.

Charles Mayer Steps In

Charles F Mayer, a Baltimore merchant, took over the B&O Presidency for the next seven years. An administrator, rather than a railroad operating man, he nevertheless contributed greatly to the expansion of the B&O. During his Presidency, a second lake port with vast terminal facilities at Cleveland was tied into the B&O system. Mayer also added a third Atlantic Ocean terminal, in addition to those at Baltimore and Philadelphia, by completing a bridge over the Arthur Kill to Staten Island in the New York harbor area. Partial ownership of the Staten Island properties had been purchased by the B&O some time before, but this bridge had to be built before they could be used to advantage. This third gateway to the Atlantic provided the capability of delivering huge volumes of freight directly to ocean-going vessels, and paved the way for a much-increased volume of foreign trade over B&O lines.

New rolling stock was purchased, and other improvements were added. President Mayer stretched new lines into the coal fields of West Virginia to capture increased soft coal haulage against very stiff competition from other railroads. He rebuilt the bridge at Harper's Ferry, to eliminate a bad curve, and increased control of the Staten Island lines. Also under Mayer, new yards and terminals at Brunswick and Cumberland, Maryland; Glenwood, Pennsylvania, and Benwood, West Virginia were built. Improvements were also made on the Baltimore-Chicago route.

Altogether during his administration, President Mayer built 178 miles of new line, absorbed 743 miles of line from other roads, increased the B&O's locomotive fleet from 755 to 890, and increased the car fleet from 27,108 to 27,320 units.

1432

THE TURN OF THE CENTURY

The Gay Nineties

The winds of change continued to blow, and the 'Gay Nineties' had arrived. It was an era that, at one and the same time, brought an end to the long day of the draft animal and horse-powered vehicle, and was the dawn of a new epoch of electricity and diesel power, of the automobile, the airplane and streamlined 100 mph trains. Over the horizon of the then-mysterious future would also come wars of unimagined scope, the nightmarish power of nuclear weapons and, most astonishing of all, mankind on Earth's Moon.

The naive excitement of the harbingers of the age to come threaded its way through the 1890s. Henry Ford built his first automobile in 1893, and the Stanley Steamer appeared four years later. The Wright brothers at Dayton, Ohio—bicycle mechanics by trade—became interested in aircraft that were self-propelled, and soon, in 1903, they produced an airplane that would fly of its own power. The US battleship *Maine* was blown up in Havana Harbor on 15 February 1898, precipitating the Spanish-American War. James J Hill, Edward H Harriman and Collis P Huntington were great and hallowed names in railroading.

Growth and a Tunnel at Baltimore

From as far back as the Civil War, US railroads had expanded at a rapid rate. Year after year, the total mileage increased—from 30,626 in 1860 to 53,922 in 1870; to 93,267 in 1880, and to 167,191 in 1890. Only 31,000 miles of line were built between 1890 and 1900, but with the turn of the century, the rate of expansion again increased. Between 1900 and 1910, the total length of rail lines in the US grew from 198,964 to 249,992 miles.

The Royal Blue Line of the Baltimore & Ohio Railroad had been inaugurated in July of 1890—four years after the completion of the B&O tracks to Philadelphia. From there, Reading and Jersey Central tracks were used by B&O trains into Jersey City. The top train of the Royal Blue Line was the *Royal Limited*, an all-Pullman parlor car train that was inaugurated in 1898, and covered the distance between Washington and Jersey City in five hours.

As long as the B&O had been operating to Philadelphia and New York—both located in its North Sector—there had been a serious bottleneck at Baltimore. There was no physical connection between the main line from the West and the lines to the North: through cars had to be ferried from one terminal to the other, across the neck of Baltimore Harbor. This was a time-consuming operation, and it was irritating to passengers and railroaders alike.

During the Garrett administration, a means of connecting these lines had often been considered but never carried out, as it would entail great effort. By the 1890s, Baltimore was a large and crowded city, with a population of 434,439 and high property values. The task of building railroad tracks across its very center—and this was the basis of the Garrett administration's plan to connect the West and North routes—involved massive engineering, legal and financial problems. At one time, acquisition of ground for an elevated rail connection

actually had been initiated, but the threat of damage suits by owners of property which was adjacent to the planned right-of-way caused that project to be abandoned.

In 1889, plans for a 'Belt Line' railroad were announced. The Belt Line solved the problem of linking the two routes by tunneling under downtown Baltimore from Camden Station, which served the Western tracks, to the northern part of the city. From there, the Belt Line swept eastward to join the tracks to Philadelphia.

In the tunnel, new electric locomotives, which represented considerable improvements over Dr Page's experimental model of 1851, were to pull the steam locomotives and their trains—thus eliminating the smoke and fumes that made railroad tunnels dangerous in those days. In addition, the tunnel was to be lighted with electricity. Both of these electrical installations were engineering innovations.

At the northern end of the tunnel, upon a lot that had long served as the depot of the old Northern Central Railroad (which ran northward from Baltimore to Pennsylvania), the B&O built a magnificent new station named Mount Royal, with a unique Norman-style clock tower. This historic station was to serve for many years, along with downtown Camden Station—these being the two B&O depots in the railroad's 'home town.'

The first steam-powered passenger train was operated over the Belt Line Railroad on 1 May 1895. In June, the first of the General Electric locomotives went into service to haul trains through the tunnel, marking the first practical use of electric motive power on any railroad in the United States.

Receivership

Despite the popular conception of that decade, there were troubles aplenty. For the 'Gay Nineties' also was a period of financial panic and depression, of unemployment and bankruptcy, and one of the most severe economic disturbances in the history of the United States to that time: with the Depression of 1893, the Baltimore & Ohio was forced to limit expenses. Except for the completion of the Belt Line, there was no expansion in those dark days. Even the financing of necessary everyday maintenance became a problem. The physical plant of the B&O deteriorated as the economic situation became increasingly severe.

With the failure in 1893 of Baring Brothers' banking firm of London, one of the principal financial supporters of the Baltimore & Ohio was gone, and President Mayer faced the most trying time of his tenure as B&O President. The total revenues of the B&O dropped appallingly from 1892 to 1896. In the stormy economic seas, the railroad hit the shoals of receivership on 29 February 1896. One month before this, Mr Mayer had resigned.

John K Cowen and Oscar G Murray were appointed receivers. The railroad was fortunate; Mr Cowen's association with the B&O dated from 1872. He succeeded Mr Mayer as President of the road. Mr Murray, after a long apprenticeship on western railroads and more advanced

Engines of the 1890s. *Previous page:* A Vauclain Compound 4-6-0 'Ten Wheeler.' *At right, from the top down:* A 4-6-0 of B&O subsidiary Baltimore & Ohio South Western; a B&O Consolidation; and a 4-4-0 American of B&O subsidiary Cincinnati, Hamilton & Dayton.

Leonor F Loree *(above)*, the B&O's President from 1901 – 04. *At left:* The B&O Marine Terminal (shown here in the 1940s — compare with page 61) in Baltimore Harbor was the site of much growth.

training on the Big Four and the Chesapeake & Ohio, had come to the B&O in 1896 as Vice President.

Immediately, the receivers set to work to improve the physical condition of the road, to renovate the rolling stock and to place orders for the great amount of additional equipment that was needed to handle the vast freight business. Within three years, some 28,000 freight cars, 16 new locomotives, and 310 passenger and other cars were added to the rolling stock.

Millions of dollars were spent for new rails, crossties and ballast. The investment proved sound. From the 1896 figures of $24 million, gross earnings jumped to nearly $36 million by 1900. The receivership, therefore, was ended after three years.

The Pennsylvania Railroad's Leonor Loree

Leonor F Loree was installed as President of the B&O by the Pennsylvania Railroad in 1901, following the purchase of 40 percent of the B&O's stock by the 'Pennsy.' Loree had been with the Pennsylvania Railroad for 18 years, and was an able railroad man, due to the Pennsy's belief in having as executives only those who had a thorough working knowledge of the railroad.

At this time, the B&O consisted of 3221 miles of main line, one-fourth of this being double-tracked. It had a huge fleet of rolling stock, and the gross earnings, including those of the B&O Southwestern, had climbed to nearly $48 million for the fiscal year of 1901. The B&O Southwestern system itself had begun with the combin-

ing of the Marietta & Cincinnati Railroad and the Hillsborough & Cincinnati Railroad. To these, in 1893, was added the Ohio & Mississippi Railroad, which had trackage to St Louis. After the turn of the century, all of had been brought into the B&O system.

Mr Loree held the Presidency until 1904. His achievements were varied and many, including a successful effort to expand and develop the system so that it could handle the B&O's now-greatly increased freight traffic, and to facilitate the movement of Pennsy rolling stock on B&O lines. To aid the efficiency of freight movements, he developed new interchange freight yards at Keyser and Fairmont, West Virginia; at Holloway, Ohio; and at Connellsville and New Castle, Pennsylvania. He built new shops and engine houses, added to the double tracking and eliminated many bad grades and curves.

B&O President Loree purchased the Ohio River Railroad, which ran south from Wheeling through Parkersburg to Huntington, West Virginia. He also increased the Baltimore & Ohio's stock holdings in the Cleveland, Lorain & Wheeling Railroad and the Philadelphia and Reading — the latter, in turn, owning part of the Central Railroad of New Jersey. He also invested in several other railroads.

Leonor F Loree put into service the first Mallet compound locomotives ever to be used in the United States. These large engines were designed to haul the heavy freight trains of the B&O over the steep mountain grades of its main lines.

With the invocation of the Sherman Anti-Trust Act by President Theodore Roosevelt in 1902, the Pennsylvania Railroad was forced to begin releasing its majority interest of the B&O, and the B&O began a slow progress down the road to independence. President Loree resigned in 1904, and was succeeded in the B&O Presidency by Oscar G Murray, the railroad's former co-receiver.

Washington Union Station

Many long years of dissatisfaction with the state of railroad facilities in Washington, DC, forced the most enraged citizen of them all — none other than US President Theodore Roosevelt — to impress upon Congress the need to impress upon the chief culprits, namely, the Pennsylvania Railroad and the Baltimore & Ohio Railroad, the need to build a single rail facility for the esthetic edification and just plain old convenience of railroad passengers coming into and leaving the capital city. This led, in 1903, to the passage of a Congressional act to facilitate the construction in the nation's capital of a station to be owned by both the B&O and Pennsylvania Railroads.

Prior to this, each of the railroads had its own station. The new terminal, 'Washington Union Station,' was built according to the plans of David H Burnham, a renowned Chicago architect. It was destined to be one of the outstanding buildings in the nation's capital, with its main concourse of 630 feet by 210 feet, its tremendous waiting room and 22 tracks for arriving and departing trains of every railroad that came into Washington. Completed late in 1907, at a cost of more than $20 million, Washington Union Station was first used by Baltimore & Ohio Train Number 10, en route from the West to New York on 27 October 1907.

THE WILLARD
ADMINISTRATION

Daniel Willard

The 31-year term of the 14th President of the Baltimore & Ohio began before World War I, and ended as a second and still greater World War was beginning. It was a time of boom and bust, and of many ups and downs — for the nation as well as for the railroad that Daniel Willard headed.

Mr Willard's Presidency began with a period of rapid expansion and improvement, then followed years that saw the B&O and all other US railroads taken over by the government during the First World War. After the war, the railroads were returned to private management in extremely poor physical and financial condition. The postwar prosperity was followed by a slight depression, and this was followed in turn by a boom period that was unprecedented in US history.

Any thoughts of lasting prosperity were cruelly dashed by the stock market crash of 1929. The subsequent depression of the early Thirties drove American industry, including the railroads, to the fiscal wall, and was so extensive that it was and still is called the 'Great Depression.' Even with these crises past, the railroads entered upon years of struggle to recover from the accumulated ravages of extended periods of poor maintenance during the war and the Great Depression. Adding to these difficulties was, of course, the rollercoaster economic climate that has characterized this century as a whole.

Daniel Willard was born in Vermont in 1861, and he started his railroad career in 1879 as a track laborer on the Vermont Central Railroad. Later he transferred to the Connecticut & Passumpsic Rivers Railroad as a fireman, in the hope that he could move up to become an engineer — which he did.

Over a long period, he worked for two western railroads in many different jobs, rising rapidly. He came to the B&O for the first time in 1899 as assistant general manager under Frederick D Underwood, who achieved great fame as a railroad man and who was then the operating Vice President of the B&O. Willard followed Underwood to the Erie in 1901, and later moved on alone to the Chicago, Burlington & Quincy as its Operating Vice President. He returned to the B&O on 1 January 1910, to be its President. An 'operations' man, Willard was interested in increasing the efficiency of the system and improving its services. The new President first set about placing his road in shape to handle the increasing amount of freight that the second decade of this century offered. He borrowed $62 million so that he could regrade and double-track the right-of-way, improve and add to the locomotive power and car fleet, and build new terminals and shops.

The elimination of the bottleneck at Doe Gulley Tunnel on the main line east of Cumberland cost $6 million in itself. For Willard personally had noted that freight trains waiting to pass through the tunnel were lined up at each entrance. To break the bottleneck, the whole top was cut off the tunnel, and the trackbed was widened, and a four-track line was laid into it. At the same time, the 17 miles of track between Cumberland and Cherry Run, on which the tunnel was located, were cut down to 11 miles by the building of a double-track short line. This was called the 'Magnolia Cut-Off,' and it served to speed up

freight movements in the upper part of the Potomac Valley.

Improvements, Disasters and Public Service

Other bottlenecks were eliminated, and Willard set about double tracking many sections of the main line. Some of these tasks were accomplished by the autumn of 1917, just after America entered the First World War, and their importance to the war effort was considerable. Other early improvements completed by Willard included a new Susquehanna River bridge at the head of Chesapeake Bay; a new stone arch viaduct across the Brandywine River at Wilmington, Delaware; a $2 million bridge across the Big Miami River west of Cincinnati, and another over the Allegheny River at Pittsburgh; and two smaller bridges across the Monongahela River at Lumberport and the Grafton River in West Virginia.

In his first 18 years as chief executive, Willard spent nearly $150 million to modernize the system. He increased the B&O locomotive fleet by 33 percent, the freight car fleet by 25 percent and the passenger car fleet by 50 percent. The majority of cars of all types were changed over from wood to steel.

Along with these material improvements, President Willard added greatly to the standing and the prestige of the road in the mind of the public — by encouraging an attitude, on the part of the railroad and its employees, of civic good will. At the very beginning of the Willard administration, there was an opportunity for the B&O to provide an early demonstration of the 'good neighbor' policy that was a high priority on Mr Willard's administrative program.

The B&O in the twentieth century. *At left:* Daniel Willard, B&O President from 1910–41. *Above: Old Maude,* the B&O's first Mallet articulated locomotive—part of the Loree legacy. *Below:* This 4-4-2 Atlantic passenger engine became part of the B&O with the acquisition of the Buffalo & Susquehanna in 1929. *Previous page:* A veteran Ten Wheeler in a service stop at Pittsburgh in the 1940s.

Devastating floods occurred in Ohio and Indiana, continuing their destructive rampages from the end of March through the month of April 1913. In the two afflicted states, more than 700 people lost their lives and many thousands were made homeless. The railroads suffered greatly as well—scores of bridges were destroyed, telegraph poles and wires were downed, and right-of-ways were covered with water and washed out. All of the railroads serving central and southern Ohio were badly damaged by the raging waters.

More than 3000 miles of B&O trackage were put out of service, and it was 12 days before even main line service could be restored. The property damage on the B&O, including the Cincinnati, Hamilton and Dayton Railroad (which it then owned), totaled over $4 million. The B&O also estimated that it had lost almost $2 million worth of traffic.

While its service was interrupted, the Baltimore & Ohio used the lines of a railroad in northern Ohio—not only to move regular traffic, but also to bring in supplies and doctors, nurses and other emergency who were sorely needed by the many suffering flood victims.

On many other occasions, the B&O has played similar roles—during floods, epidemics and in many localized catastrophies. Locomotives, linked to local facilities, have provided steam, heat and power when community power systems have been disrupted. On one occasion, a quantity of B&O fuel oil was given to orchard growers in a midwestern state, when a sudden frost threatened their fruit crops. The 'good neighbor' policy has been extended to individuals as well, and memorable incidents abound,

including an emergency operation aboard a B&O crack passenger train.

To formalize the cooperative attitude of the B&O, and to make it a promise to the public, B&O President Willard announced in 1916:

'It will be the policy of the Baltimore & Ohio Railroad Company, first of all, to endeavor to do efficiently all the things that a public servant should do. It will earnestly try to satisfy the reasonable requirements of the public for transportation.

'It is our desire that people living along our lines should feel that the Baltimore & Ohio Railroad is a good neighbor. For instance, if they are visited by fire, flood or epidemic, etc, they should instinctively call upon us first for assistance, because of our potential strength and our willingness to help them.

'We will treat our shippers and passengers with absolute fairness and with sympathetic consideration. When we make a contract, we will do our utmost to live up to it. We want to deal with our patrons as two honorable men deal with each other.'

The First World War

World War I began on 28 July 1914, when Austria declared war upon Serbia. Other nations plunged into the war in quick succession; soon all of Europe was aflame. In 1916, the British passenger ship *Lusitania* was sunk by a German submarine, and hundreds of its passengers, including many Americans, were drowned. Considering this an outrage, America threw its hat into

Above: A B&O E-60 class 2-8-0 freight engine and its train, photographed in 1946 near Ansonia, Pennsylvania. Engines of a similar design saw much service with the B&O during World War I.

the ring in the spring of 1917.

American railroads rolled up their sleeves and went to war. The B&O's President Willard was by that time considered to be one of the nation's finest railroad executives, and was named by US President Woodrow Wilson to serve on an advisory commission of the Council of National Defense. The first problem to be faced — and solved — was the movement of large quantities of West Virginia coal to the Pacific Coast bases of the US Navy. These bases had been supplied by coal ships sailing via the Panama Canal, but with the exigencies of war, this method was now seen as too slow, and further, as not delivering coal in sufficient quantity.

To attain quicker and more abundant delivery, the cooperation of railroads nationwide was achieved in order to organize a vast army of hopper cars. Transcontinental routes, over which the trainloads of coal could move westward on priority schedules, were then plotted. Upon delivering their coal, the empty trains returned for more coal over alternate routes, to keep the 'main line' clear for express deliveries.

Other problems rose on every side. A closeknit nationwide rail organization was needed. The Council of National Defense set up the Railroads' War Board, which consisted of Fairfax Harrison of the Southern Railway, Samuel Rea of the Pennsylvania, Julius Kruttschnitt of the Southern Pacific, Hale Holden of the Burlington and Howard Elliott of the Northern Pacific. Willard, as head of

the advisory commission, was an ex-officio member of the rail board, which had authority over all of the properties of 635 American railroad companies.

Thus, a unified nationwide railroad — after a manner of speaking — was made available to the wartime government. It was a vast organization with $17.5 billion worth of property, 250 thousand miles of lines, 2.3 million freight cars, 54,000 passenger cars and 64,000 locomotives.

As a member of the team, the B&O helped carry war materials to the eastern seaports for shipment overseas. Other hundreds of thousands of tons of freight had to be moved within the country — raw material for manufacturing had to be moved to the factories that would use them, and completed products had to be moved from factories to civilian and military users. Millions of men, newly inducted into the Army, had to be transported to training camps, three of the largest of these — Fort Meade, near Baltimore; Camp Sherman, at Chillicothe, Ohio; and Camp Taylor, at Louisville — being located on B&O lines.

After their brief training was completed, the new citizen soldiers, fitted in mesh knaki, entrained for the seaports for shipment to France. Here again the B&O played a big part, for it had lines in service to all three major gateways to Europe: Baltimore Harbor, Philadelphia Harbor and New York Harbor.

Competing with other war industries for materials and labor, the railroads found themselves handicapped by rising costs. Losing men to the services, despite their own heavy manpower needs, the railroads fought against the increasing strain with fewer men than were sufficient. The vast wartime tonnages of men and freight required more and more rolling stock — until the railroads no longer could find enough to meet the combined demands of the war industries, the military and the civilians.

Government Control

The car shortage was increased by reason of the fact that many cars were used for 'storage' purposes over long periods at seaports. While this particular problem was solved by the cooperation engendered by the formation of the Railroads' War Board, it was, as the saying goes, 'only the beginning of trouble.' The US government had long distrusted the seemingly untrammeled power of the railroads — and difficulties such as the car shortage, especially in time of national emergency, were ample stimulus for government intervention — and control.

Late in 1917, President Wilson decided that the majority of these problems could be solved by having the government run the railroads, and on 28 December of that year, William G McAdoo, Wilson's Secretary of the Treasury, was named 'Director General of Railroads.' Under him, a large bureaucracy was set up to control railroad traffic and administer railroad business.

Government control of the railroads lasted through 1920, and had a damaging effect in many ways. Right-of-ways and rolling stock deteriorated, due to the government's low-maintenance policies, and expenses were allowed to mount until they exceeded income. These problems could be overcome — but the maturing century would present, time and again, such difficulty for the

Above left: This 4-6-2 Pacific was acquired when the B&O bought the BR&P in 1929 (see text). The 0-8-0 in the 1939 photo *at left* was operated by the B&O subsidiary, B&O Chicago Terminal Company. *Above:* A B&O 4-6-0 engages in a late steam-era switch operation.

nation's railroads that the circumstances of the second decade would be a bad omen for many.

After the War

During the postwar period, the Baltimore & Ohio organized a 'Cooperative Shop Plan.' It was the forerunner of many similar plans to give industrial workers a chance to make suggestions to their companies for improving methods and equipment. Cooperative committees to represent the railroad management and the Federated Shop Crafts were organized in each shop, and they met twice a month to discuss suggestions made by the employees. Over a period of years, tens of thousands of suggestions have been received—and most of them adopted. As a result, better maintenance and housekeeping of railroad property, increased efficiency and economy in the shops and higher morale among the shop workers have been effected.

Other organizations designed to improve the relationship between the railroad's management and the employees had been founded in 1880. This was the Baltimore & Ohio Employees' Relief Association, later renamed the Relief Department. It was set up to assist employees in the event of sickness or injury, and to aid them in buying homes and to handle pensions. It also served as a bank for employees' savings in the days before bank deposits were government insured.

Nearing the end of its first 100 years, the B&O was still growing, mostly by a process of absorbing smaller railroads. Just before the entry of the United States into World War I, the B&O had purchased the Coal & Coke Railroad—thus extending its lines into Charleston, the capital of West Virginia. At the same time, the B&O organized the Toledo & Cincinnati Railroad to integrate a large portion of its rail lines in Ohio. In 1920, the Morgantown & Kingwood Railroad was bought, and six years later, the B&O took over the Cincinnati, Indianapolis & Western, adding Indianapolis to the cities served by its ribbons of steel. In 1927, the B&O attained a 40 percent ownership of the Western Maryland Railway, later increasing this to 43 percent.

The late 1920s were years of many innovations and improvements in B&O services. A considerable stock ownership of the Buffalo, Rochester & Pittsburgh brought that road into the B&O system.

THE FAIR OF THE IRON HORSE

A Grand Celebration

The most important public event concerning the B&O during the 1920s was the celebration of the grand old railroad's 100th birthday, and plans were laid accordingly by the B&O chief executive.

In 1925, B&O President Willard hired Edward Hungerford, a journalist and public relations specialist, to be the chief engineer of the B&O's birthday party, slated to occur two years from then. After much research and consideration, it was decided by Hungerford and his committee that the celebration should occur in two parts. The first segment would honor the actual centenary birthday of the railroad, 28 February 1927, and would be an invitation-only dinner and celebration.

Part of the consideration for the second, public, segment of the celebration was that of venue. If it was going to be truly large enough to honor the progress of such a vast undertaking as the B&O, it should take place where there is room enough not only for the truly spectacular, but for multitudes of people to be awed by 'the truly spectacular.'

Of course, it would have to occur outside. That meant that the date had to be set for fair weather; therefore, the opening date was set for 24 September 1927 — in the autumn, when conditions are cool, crisp and dry. Plans were laid, upon consultation with President Willard, to make this public celebration stupendous, and to charge nothing for admission. The celebration was to run for two weeks — until 8 August.

This extravagant culmination of the centenary year was advertised as 'The Centenary Exhibition and Pageant of the Baltimore & Ohio,' which speedily became known in the vernacular as 'The Fair of the Iron Horse.' No matter which appellation one used for the exhibition (the latter soon dominated all but official B&O references to it), it was to be a truly colossal public exhibition.

A Historical Dinner

The private centenary dinner and celebration took place at Baltimore's Lyric Theater, and was attended by 964 men, among whom were all 150 members of the Maryland legislature, politicos and officeholders from the nation's capitol, labor union officials, B&O top brass, presidents of several other railroads, and bankers and rail officials from New York and Philadelphia, many of who were brought to the dinner in two special trains — both of which had business cars, Pullmans and B&O diners for their guests' comfort and convenience. Many, many more dignitaries wanted to attend than could actually be accomodated, and as it was, the attending crowd had to be split into two groups for the dinner portion of the event, as the Lyric Theater lacked floor space for all of them.

So, 725 guests dined at tables situated on the main floor and in several of the boxes of the theater, while the remaining 239 guests had their dinner in the ballroom of the nearby Belvedere Hotel. Since it was Prohibition, no

The fast 4-6-2 Pacific design saw service over five decades. On the *previous page*, a Pacific heads a 1940s B&O passenger train. *At right:* A B&O 2-8-0 Consolidation, equipped with high-efficiency Caprotti valve gear. This engine symbolizes the B&O's focus on quality.

alcoholic drinks were served. The dinner was planned by B&O Dining Car Manager EV Baugh, and had several courses, including green turtle soup, Chesapeake Bay diamond back terrapin, sweet potatoes, Smithfield ham, various dessert ices and cakes, cofee, ginger ale and mineral water, and more.

The dinner at the Lyric Theater was opened by an invocation given by the Reverend John Gardner Murray, Presiding Bishop of the Protestant Episcopal Churches of America. President Willard presided over the larger gathering, and B&O Vice President George Shriver was the head functionary at the Belvedere Hotel festivities. After the meal, the guests at the Belvedere filled the balcony of the Lyric for the second portion of the event.

President Willard introduced the speakers and the program in general. The keynote speech was a historical address by Newton D Baker, former US Secretary of War and a Director of the B&O since 1923. Mr Baker stated, amongst other grand sentiments, that,

'No hundred years in the history of mankind has seen greater change or greater progress. That we are a strong, coherent people; that we have been able to exploit and use the resources of the continent; that we have been able to build up a splendid civilization with a higher degree of comfort and a larger opportunity for every citizen of the republic is, in every essential part, because of the railroad system.

'Verily, the little group of men who in 1827 projected the Baltimore & Ohio were prophets of a great future and architects of a great nation.'

Maryland Governor Albert Ritchie and Baltimore Mayor Howard Jackson were also scheduled to speak, but Governor Ritchie was kept at home by illness. When the oratory was over, choral singing by the B&O Women's Music Club, and then the B&O Glee Club, was followed by a bit of theater in the form of three dramatized scenes from the early history of the B&O Railroad.

The first scene was set in the home of banker George Brown in February of 1827. A group of Baltimore business men, including Brown, gathered about a long table discussing their incipient railroad project. As the scene drew to a conclusion, a messenger burst in upon the group with the news that the Maryland legislature had just ratified the charter for their project, the B&O Railroad. There was thunderous applause.

The second scene portrayed the laying of the first stone of the B&O at Mount Clare. Exacting attention to detail marked this presentation. The third and final vignette centered on the first horse car that made daily trips on the B&O, and Peter Cooper, with a close reproduction of the *Tom Thumb*. At the close of this, the Peter Cooper character stood at stage front, seeing in a dream vision one of the B&O's powerful twentieth century steam locos hurtling along at speeds Peter Cooper wouldn't have imagined.

The entire affair was over by 11 o'clock. As the guests left, each was given one of the B&O Centenary Medals. These medals were 2.75 inches in diameter, were cast in bronze, and featured, alternately, the *Capitol Limited* or the *National Limited* encircled by the words 'One

Hundred Years — Safety – Strength — Speed.' On the other side of each medal was Peter Cooper's *Tom Thumb*, likewise encircled with the phrase '1827 – 1927 — The Baltimore and Ohio Railroad Company.' The medals were also given to B&O pensioners and employees with 40 or more years of service, plus they could be bought by the general public for $1.50.

Planning the Fair

It was now time to shore up plans for the truly massive public exhibition scheduled for September of that year. This open air extravaganza was taken very seriously by the Mayor of Baltimore and by the Governor of Maryland, who made up committees to work closely with the B&O concerning the public relations, travel logistics, lodging and general safety questions concerning the Fair.

The basic plan was to have a pageant of locomotives of all kinds — hence, the 'Iron Horse' appellation. Naturally, a goodly chunk of ground was necessary for such a spectacle, and several were investigated. The City of Baltimore offered the use of one of its parks — which was generous, but the logistics of altering the park for the exhibition, and then restoring it afterward precluded the site. A racetrack between Baltimore and Washington was the next likely venue, but this also proved impracticable. Finally, a 1000 acre tract of land, located eight

The B&O took pride in their rolling stock. Below left, one of the great Pacifics heads a train out of Chicago. *Below:* A B&O Ten Wheeler and train stops for water on the Landenburg Branch.

miles out of Baltimore near the town of Halethrope, proved to be the place that was needed.

Ironically, this land had been in the B&O's 'back pocket' all the time, having been purchased 50 years earlier by B&O President John Garrett. The land was ideally situated, near the intersection of the main lines between Baltimore and Washington and New York and Florida.

The Fair: Built for History

First of all, the pageant engineers laid down a 6000 foot loop of track for the loco exhibits, and inside this, a loop of dirt road for other transportation exhibits. Facing these was a grandstand capable of holding 12,048 people. The canopy for this stand featured one of the largest pieces of canvas ever fabricated in the US. Just behind the grandstand was the main line of the B&O, with a special station built just for exhibition traffic.

Across the grounds from the grandstand was the large, open stretch of ground known as the Court of Honor, which formed a background for the pageant when viewed from the stands. This was flanked on either side by the Allied Services Building and the Traffic Building. Behind the court was the most important building of the exhibition, the Hall of Transportation, which was 504 feet long by 62 feet wide. These buildings were all designed in Colonial style and were built predominately of brick with wood trim. Their roofs, as were all the roofs of the exhibition structures, including the grandstand canopy,

were royal blue and white — the traditional B&O colors. The Hall of Transportation was topped by a tower in which hung the oldest bell on the B&O. This bell was taken from the belfry of the Ellicott City passenger station. Since 1830, it had announced the comings and goings of B&O trains. At certain times during the fair, this venerable old bell was rung again.

The B&O's long-standing stewardship of some of its obsolete equipment paid off big for the display at the Fair. Almost unique among America's utility-conscious railroads, the B&O had stored — rather than scrapped — its earliest, historically valuable, locomotives and cars. At the beginning of the year, these antiques were taken out of storage in Martinsburg, transported to a roundhouse in Baltimore and there were painstakingly refurbished, and come show time, such venerable B&O locos as the *Atlantic*, the *Thomas Jefferson*, the *William Mason* and the *Thatcher Perkins* gleamed anew to the fascination of the thronging crowds.

Much of this collection was due to the efforts of one man, Major JG Pangborn, a traffic officer of the B&O around the turn of the century, who devoted his life to the study of the line's early history. He instigated the salvaging of the early locos for the 1893 Chicago World's Fair. In addition to this, later engines were added as the years rolled on. Major Pangborn built full scale wood models of other famous locomotives from around the world, for a total of 32 models in all. The entire collection was shown at the Fair of the Iron Horse, and the models were placed prominently on a double track running the

At left: A view of the grand 'Fair of the Iron Horse' — as it was popularly known. The grandstand is on the far side. Long before and after the Fair, the B&O had demanded the finest motive power, including such as this 2-10-0 Decapod *(below)*, of the late 1940s.

interior length of the Hall of Transportation. These were supplemented with hundreds of large pictures detailing the development and evolution of locomotives, cars, track and appliances worldwide.

Many and varied were the railroads that loaned historical equipment for the Fair. Long-standing rivalries could not dim the fervor to add to this magnificent exhibition, for the Pennsylvania Railroad loaned the Camden & Amboy's *John Bull*, which was the first locomotive on that line (and the earliest locomotive on any Pennsy affiliate line); the New York Central sent over its replica of the *DeWitt Clinton*, which first operated in 1831 on the Mohawk & Hudson. Modern locos were included, too, as the *George V* of Great Britain's Great Western Railway was sent over from its home land, and the Pennsy, the NYC and other railroads sent a few prime examples of their latest in steam-powered, smoke breathing cast iron muscle.

The Exhibits

The Hall of Transportation contained, besides the Pangborn models, two scale models of the B&O physical plant, illustrating the railroad's history and progress. One of these was a 'time capsule' that exactingly detailed the B&O Harpers Ferry facility as it stood just before the Civil War. The other was 250-foot long trip through time, showing the railroad's development through the years. Also, there were other exhibits tracing the development and innovative history of such important railroad equipment as brakes, signals, tracks, couplers, stokers, injectors, bridges and wheel trucks. The numerous companies that manufactured the various items cooperated fully in supplying historical data, information and other needed assistance in order that the exhibit be a success.

The building also held many miniature models of railroad around the world, including examples from Egypt, Russia and elsewhere. The models detailed bridges, cars and engines, and such other mechanical phenomena as might be of interest. A series of 10 short tracks in front of the Hall exemplified the development of trackbed and rails since the birth of the B&O.

The Traffic Building was a display of the various means through which the railroad had sought, and served, its passengers through the years. Early tickets, waybills and advertisements were on display, and again, scale models were used with great effect. There were scale models of the Mount Royal passenger station, the entire Central Headquarters building in Baltimore and a bas-relief map of the entire territory traversed by the system. This was so well detailed, it included minitures of the various terminals along the line. A working model of the state-of-the-art wharf setup and loading machinery at the B&O's coal facility at Curtis Bay, and a very large model of the new grain elevator at Locust Point (including its automatic belt carriers and wharves) occupied the center of the building.

The Allied Services Building contained a huge map of the B&O system, painted in antique style by George Illian. There were also exhibits prepared by the US Post Office; Railway Express; Western Union; and American Telephone and Telegraph Company. Still more exhibits depicted the modern accounting methods of the B&O, but also the many charitable and public-welfare projects

that the firm had undertaken. The railway mail and express services also gave demonstrations of their service in actual modern cars on the outdoor tracks. The Pullman Company also provided an open-air exhibit that included progressive examples that ran from a sleeping car of 1859 up to and including their most modern project, the entire train of the B&O's premier passenger flyer, the *Capitol Limited.*

The buildings mentioned so far comprised the principal exhibition structures at the Fair. There was also the General Washington Inn, which was a replication of a tavern the likes of which one found along the way back in the 1830s. This served as an administration and press headquarters. A 400-seat coffee house that served an average of 9000 meals per day, and a building devoted to exhibitions of local and state culture. Public health, hospital, fire department and other necessary buildings were also in evidence. A huge round booth—known for the duration of the Fair as the 'Roundhouse,' served as a central souvenir stand, sort of *grande dame* with full skirts amidst a flock of smaller stands hawking sandwiches, ice cream, soft drinks and cigars.

A Parade of Transportation History

There were also cars that served as dressing rooms and costume storage for the actors who played in the pageant. The many floats that participated in the grand show were kept under a circus tent when not in use. And, of course, there were facilities for maintenance and fueling of the many locomotives that rightfully dominated this Fair of the Iron Horse.

This brings us to the pageant itself. The pageant occurred everyday but Sunday for the duration of the Fair, and drew so well that the closing day was reset for 16 October of that year. The story of the growth of the railroad was told quietly and exactly in the exhibits, but it was made far more lively and picturesque in the pageant, which featured actors, actresses and mobile floats. The pageant flowed in a single direction around the loop track, from the dressing rooms over near the Hall of Transportation, past the grand stand and other spectator positions, and back again to the dressing rooms.

The dramatic procession took an hour and a quarter to

At left: A pair of Pacifics get a passenger train underway fast.

wagon; one example each of four- and six-horse stage coaches; and a gentleman's carriage transporting none other than the Great Compromiser himself, Henry Clay, over the old National Road to Washington; and assorted folk riding along on their various travels.

Of course, there was a faithful and highly detailed representation of the first B&O parade, that festive spectacle in the streets of old Baltimore that preceded the laying of the 'first stone' so long ago, complete with reproductions of the four floats that were used in that historic celebration. That began a new chapter in the story—the coming of the Iron Horse itself. There was the experimental sail-car, the treadmill car and the horse car. Each bore its passengers with alacrity. And then came the *Tom Thumb*, a full replication (product of the Mount Clare Shops) chugging along under its own steam, and with Peter Cooper at the controls! Likewise came the *York*, also a reproduction wrought at the Mount Clare Shops.

The *Atlantic* and the *Thomas Jefferson* which followed were the originals, though, and they moved along under their own power 'most smartly.' The *Atlantic* hauled two reproductions of the Richard Imlay-designed double-decker coaches that rode the B&O rails in 1831. These elegant old coaches carried a full complement of ladies and gentlemen dressed in the highest fashion of their bygone day.

Then, hauling two flour cars of the kind that transported tons of flour on the early B&O lines, came the *Lafayette*, which had been renamed the *William Galloway* (specifically for exhibition at the Fair) in honor of a distinguished B&O locomotive engineer of 'the old days.' Following this was a procession of original antiques including the *Memnon*, the *William Mason*, the *Thatcher Perkins* (hauling a train of small Civil War era passenger coaches, painted a festive yellow) and various others, many in the dazzling paint jobs that often distinguished locomotives of their day.

A Camel named the *Ross Winans*, hauling three coal hoppers and two sheet iron box cars was followed by the *JC Davis* and the *AJ Cromwell*; and then followed *Number 545*, a Consolidation type locomotive built in 1888 by AJ Cromwell, who succeeded JC Davis as Chief of Motive Power; and after that, several other locomotives of historic note from the same period.

Interspersed with this parade of nineteenth century locomotive history were various float-vignettes depicting a meeting of leading Baltimore citizens at the house of George Brown, during the planning of the B&O; a team of US Army Corps of Engineers officers making the first surveys for the railroad; the arrival of Abraham Lincoln in Washington for his first inauguration; the destruction of the B&O's tracks by both militaries of the Civil War; and the advent of the first B&O electric locomotives in the late nineteenth century.

The next segment of the parade was given over to the country in which the locomotive originated, Great Britain. A float, complete with a female figure who represented Britannia, bore thematic material pertaining to the first successful locomotive, the Stephenson *Rocket*. This float was followed by the *King George V*, sent over to the Fair by the oldest British railway to operate

pass a given point, and would have stretched more than four miles if all of its constituent parts were laid out in a straight line. Each day, the band would march up to and take its place upon the bandstand. Then the pageant began, headed by the B&O Glee Club riding on a float that was draped with the American flag. This and all other floats in the pageant were driven by motors hidden under its overflowing stage apron. After the Glee Club sang the 'Star Spangled Banner' to the audience in the stands, the drama began.

The pageant was set in a series of historical vignettes, each one separated from the others by the length of time it took each to traverse a certain space of track, or of road. The first vignette, meaning to show the earliest modes of transportation, featured Blackfoot Indians with heavily laden pack animals and travois trailing in the dust of the highway; then followed a float featuring the missionary and explorer Father Joliet and his entourage; then floats showing inland water transport such as primitive bateaux and an early canal boat—all appropriately manned with crew and passengers.

Then came a variety of road wagons; and a Conestoga

Above: A Pacific (rear) and a 2-8-2 Mikado approach a station in the mountains of West Virginia in 1948· similar engines were part of the Fair of the Iron Horse. *At right:* A B&O train by the Potomac.

without change of name or charter, the Great Western Railway. This four-cylinder locomotive was produced by the Great Western's own Swindon Shops, weighed 135 tons with its tender, and was one of the finest passenger locomotives in England at the time. Two Canadian locos followed; these were the *Confederation*, of Canadian National Railways, and *Number 2333* of the Canadian Pacific Railway.

Coming to a Grand Conclusion

Again appeared American locos of yore, with a recap of the grand old days of railroading. In the following order appeared the *De Witt Clinton* (circa 1831), of the old Mohawk & Hudson, on loan from the NYC, trailing three coaches full of folk costumed for the period; then the *John Bull*, of the Camden & Amboy, a contemporary of the *De Witt Clinton*, on loan from the Pennsy, and hauling a coach full of quaint passengers; the old locomotive *Satilla*, (circa 1860) of the Atlantic & Gulf, on loan from Henry Ford; and the *William Crooks* (circa 1861), the first locomotive in the Northwest, on loan from the Great Northern, hauling a baggage car and a passenger car.

Then the pageant stepped into the present, for a viewing of the NYC's then-new 4-6-4 Hudson type passenger locomotive, designed and built by that railroad, and placed in service just a few months before the Fair; and a huge Pennsy 4-6-2 Pacific, one of the premier passenger types of the steam age; and a Western Maryland coal hauler; and then the *John B Jervis*, of the Delaware &

Hudson. This was a very modern loco, with a water-tube firebox, a high pressure boiler, a rear-truck-mounted booster, and an almost nonexistent smokestack.

Modern B&O motive power was then represented by a 4-6-0 Ten Wheeler passenger hauler; a converted Mikado for passenger traffic; a 2-8-2 Mikado freight hauler; a 2-10-2 Santa Fe type; and then the grand appearance of the *Philip E Thomas*, a 4-8-2 mountain type (the original loco bearing this name was an American type) passenger loco. This engine and tender was 100 feet long, but its mighty bulk was overshadowed by the appearance of one of B&O's gigantic Mallet compounds.

So went the pageantry of the Fair of the Iron Horse. Daily attendance had averaged 50,000 per day, with a crowd of well over 100,000 on 15 October, with the Fair receiving some spillover from a Notre Dame football game that was in progress that day. For the extended three weeks that the Fair was in operation, total attendance was more than 1.3 million, with 270,000 railroad tickets to the Fairgrounds having been sold.

After the Fair had closed, its sounding note resonated long and deep; it had been an event of celebration, yet it also struck — long and powerfully — the note of change, and change again. Who knew what the decades yet to come would bring? Those who went home with mementoes and brochures knew for certain that they would have 'something to tell their grandchildren about some day.'

THE GREAT DEPRESSION

The Stock Market Crash

The stock market crash of 1929 heralded the unprecedented business depression of the 1930s. However hard it hit at first, the *full* effects of the 'Great Depression' were not to be felt generally by US industry for several years. When they were, the US railroads were among the heaviest industrial sufferers, for the railroads were the main transportation agency of US industry; and when industry had slowed nearly to a standstill, the railroad freight business suffered accordingly.

By 1932, the total tonnage carried by US railroads had dropped to less than half of what it had been in the boom year of 1929. From 1932 on, however, the picture improved and the railroads' business increased steadily — except for a slight recession in 1938 and 1939, just before World War II.

Despite the financial vagaries of the Great Depression and the national air of pessimism brought on by it, the B&O continued to look to the future. In many ways it led the nation in doing so. For instance, in 1930, the B&O introduced the world's first successfully air-conditioned car, a diner called the *Martha Washington* — and, several months later, the first cars with individual reclining seats were placed in service by the B&O.

The first train in America to be completely air-conditioned was the B&O's streamlined, all-coach *Columbian*, which was put into service between Washington and New York in 1931. In 1932, the first air-conditioned sleeping car train, the *National Limited*, was installed on the B&O between New York and St Louis.

The first nationwide radio broadcast from a moving train was made in March 1932, when the Columbia Broadcasting Company transmitted a feature from a B&O train traveling between Baltimore and Washington. Experimenting in lightweight equipment, the B&O in 1935 acquired two streamlined, high-speed passenger trains, one of aluminum alloy and the other of lightweight steel. One of these operated over the Alton Railroad (which the B&O then owned), between Chicago and St Louis; and the other saw use over B&O trackage between New York and Washington.

The first self-contained diesel-electric road locomotive to be used on a long-distance passenger train in the US was placed in service on the B&O in August 1935. Additional diesel-electric locomotives were added to the B&O's passenger fleet in 1937. That year, the first 'Stewardess-Nurses' went to work on B&O trains, and the B&O's first road freight diesel operated in 1942. Dieselization would come to completely supercede steam power on very nearly every railroad in the US within a few decades.

However, during the worst of the Depression, US railroads, including the B&O, took in so little money that they could not maintain their properties satisfactorily. Also, these low earnings sometimes prevented the railroads from paying even the interest they owed on their debts.

The B&O was in just such a position. In 1938, it found that it had earned only enough to cover 60 percent of its

fixed charges—the interest on the money it owed. Congress thereupon unanimously passed a law under which the B&O—with the consent of a specified proportion of its bondholders, and with the approval of the Interstate Commerce Commission and the Federal Court—put into effect a plan to postpone some of its interest payments.

Thus, the B&O was able to avoid bankruptcy until better times made it possible to pay the delayed interest. All interest eventually was paid in full. A similar financial problem arose in 1944, when more than $112 million of the B&O's debts were to mature or fall due. Again, through a similar procedure, the company adopted a plan to refinance some of these debts at lower interest rates, and to make the payment of some of the interest dependent upon earnings. In other words, if earnings in any year were not large enough to pay the interest on the debt, some of the interest payments could be postponed, but all of them had to paid in the long run.

Both of these plans worked out successfully and the B&O security holders were protected from losses they otherwise would have sustained. Through sinking funds (provided for under the plans) and in other ways, the company saved enough money to pay off a substantial amount of its bonded debt. This reduced annual interest charges and strengthened the B&O's financial position.

Previous page: A B&O coal yard in the twentieth century. *Below far left:* Machinists like this fellow assisted greatly with equipment improvements and upkeep. The B&O made many passenger service improvements in the 1930s. *Below left:* Jean Wise, a B&O Stewardess of the program that was instituted in 1939. *Below:* The B&O's *Royal Blue* steams through Holmes, Pennsylvania in the 1940s.

Thus, during and after World War II the B&O was better able to finance the modernization of its equipment and other facilities, and to increase its operating efficiency and traffic.

A Willard Farewell

Daniel Willard resigned as President on 1 June 1941, after more than 31 years in that position. He remained active as the chairman of the Board of Directors until his death in Baltimore on 6 July 1942, at the age of 81. His fellow Board members adopted a resolution upon the announcement of his death:

'His accomplishments in the field of railroading were too numerous to recount here. He was a pioneer and introduced many improvements in railroad operation, among which were air-conditioned cars and diesel locomotives.

'When he came to the Baltimore & Ohio as President on 15 January 1910, shippers were holding meetings to protest against the inadequacy of its freight facilities, and the public was critical of its passenger service. During his incumbency, the company's mileage and property investment were developed, and when he retired the railroad was rendering, as it is today, almost unexcelled service.

'His leadership in employer-employee relations was an asset not only to the Baltimore & Ohio but redounded also to the benefit of industry generally and to the country as a whole.'

B&O LOCOMOTIVES UP TO DIESELIZATION

Early Steam

At this point we might well stop to consider the state of B&O motive power through the years. Peter Cooper's *Tom Thumb* was a brave beginning, but was certainly not the powerful engine that the railroad would need to negotiate the demands of its growing trackage.

The vertical boiler 'grasshopper' locos that followed in the *Tom Thumb's* wake were an improvement, with their four vertical pushrods providing torque for the engines' four wheels (and providing the engines with their interesting monicker). Most of the grasshoppers were built by Phineas Davis, and after that pioneering locomotive builder died aboard one of his own engines in 1835, the soon-to-be-renowned Ross Winans took over Davis' Mount Clare locomotive shop with George Gillingham, and continued turning out grasshoppers until 1837.

New Types

In 1838, Winans built two engines of the 'crab' design, which were essentially grasshoppers having horizontal, as opposed to vertical, cylinders. Also, from 1837–39, B&O President McLane saw the need for heavier power than the grasshoppers could provide, and bought a number of William Norris-built horizontal boiler engines with 4-2-0 wheel placement.

Ross Winans set up his own locomotive shop in the 1840s, and produced engines there with an 0-8-0 design. These engines performed heavy freight duty well, but sometimes derailed on some of the B&O's sharper curves. They were called 'mud diggers' because of their tendency to pound the mud up between the ties as the heavy engines passed along the rails. B&O President McLane bought about a dozen of these engines in the mid-to-late 1840s.

Winans built his first 'Camel' type locomotive, an 0-8-0, in 1848. The Camel design placed the engine cab midway over the boiler and wheels. Winans built over 100 Camels for the B&O in the next nine years.

Locos on the B&O were classed according to weight in 1848, with the four classes running the gamut from 'Class 1'—at 19 and one-half to 23 and one-half tons—to 'Class 4'—at 10 to 11 tons. The former were for frieght, the latter for freight and passenger, with the intervening classes divided likewise. At that point in time, there were 57 locos on the B&O roster.

Heavier Power

Some 76 new locomotives were bought by the B&O in the first years of the 1850s, and most of these new engines were Winans Camels, which represented the standard B&O motive power up until the end of the Civil War, when the railroad bought 42 used 'American' type 4-4-0s from the federal government. Of course, there were other types of motive poqwer extant on the line during the prewar years, including some 4-4-0 'Americans,' and Camels that were not built by Ross Winans.

The B&O has always sought to maintain the most versatile fleet of locomotive power available. *Previous page:* A huge 2-10-2 Santa Fe type freight locomotive, photographed in 1947. *At right:* A late-edition Hayes Camel of 1875 (see text above), in the B&O Museum.

These non-Winans Camels were built by B&O Master of Machinery Samuel J Hayes, and were known as 'Hayes Ten Wheelers,' because this design had a wheel arrangement of 4-6-0. The leading truck greatly added stability to the Camel design, and when Henry Tyson assumed Hayes' office in 1856, he ordered 10 more of the Hayes design. This precipitated a feud between Ross Winans and Tyson as to which Camel design the B&O had a right to use. The railroad naturally sided with Tyson, and from that point on, the B&O had no more new Winans locomotives.

By 1857, the B&O had 236 locomotives, and by 1877, there were 590 locomotives on the roster, including 4-4-0 Americans, and a new batch of 4-6-0 Camels built by Master of Machinery John C Davis. In 1875, Davis built a 45-ton Mogul type (2-6-0, cab at rear) loco, the *JC Davis*, which led the way for other Moguls on the line. In the 1870s and 1880s, Consolidation type engines (2-8-0, cab at rear) were also brought into the B&O itinerary of rolling stock.

In addition to these, a dozen American type engines, of 42 tons each, and one 33 ton switch engine were also added to the lists. Many of the above engines were built at the B&O's Mount Clare shops. The construction of the Belt Line in Baltimore necessitated the addition of electric locomotives to the B&O fleet. The first of these, known as *Number One*, weighed 96 tons, and generated 56,000 lb of tractive force.

A notable 4-4-0 in B&O service was the *Director General*, a Baldwin-built engine, with 78-inch drivers, that was a B&O feature in the 1893 World's Columbian Exposition at Chicago. At that time, the *Director General* had just set a speed record of 96 mph. In 1899, the B&O had 954 locomotives (four of which were electrics).

A New Century

Under the guidance of President Leonor Loree, the B&O ordered the first Mallet type locomotive in America. This engine, built to a design originated in France by Anatole Mallet, had two sets of drivers powered by a single firebox and boiler. An 0-6-6-0, this engine weighed 167.25 tons, and generated 71,500 lb of tractive force. The engine was built by the American Locomotive Com-

pany, and was dubbed 'Old Maude,' because, although powerful, it tended to balk, like 'Maude the mule,' a popular comic strip character of the era.

The B&O would employ many more Mallets in its time, as these hefty locomotives were of great use on the steep inclines of the B&O's eastern trackage. After the turn of the century, new types of locos began to replace the old 4-4-0 Americans that had served the B&O's passeneger traffic so well for so long. Besides 4-6-0 'ten wheelers,' these newer locos also included the speedy 4-4-2 Atlantic and 4-6-2 Pacific types. In addition, more 2-8-0 Consolidations were ordered for freight service.

In 1910, B&O President Daniel Willard had convinced the B&O Board to purchase 284 locomotives to upgrade rolling stock, and in 1911, he bought 150 2-8-2 Mikado-type locos from the Baldwin Locomotive Works. These were freight engines weighing 140 tons, with 64-inch drivers and 50,000 lb of tractive force. This loco type would eventually mount to the 600 unit mark on the B&O roster, an abundance that in part was due to the equipment policies instituted by the government during, and after, World War I.

Most of the freight engines bought by the B&O during the freight service build up of the 1920s were Mikados, 2-10-2 Santa Fes, or Mallet articulated locos—this era also saw the retirement of the B&O's tried and true 2-8-0 Consolidations. The first 25 of the B&O's Santa Fe type locos had been bought from Baldwin back in 1914, and in the 1920s, 75 were bought from Baldwin, and 50 were bought from the Lima Locomotive Company. These were larger than the first B&O Santa Fes, having 64-inch drivers and developing 84,300 lb of tractive force.

Having been introduced to the B&O by Leonor Loree, the gigantic Mallet type of freight engine became a fixture on the B&O roster. Between 1927, the B&O had 135 Mallets on its lines. These were of the early 0-8-8-0 and later 2-8-8-0 wheel configurations, the largest putting out 118,000 lb of tractive force for its weight of nearly 500,000 lb.

About 50 Atlantics had been bought by the B&O in the

Below: An 1893 4-4-0 Vauclain Compound—steam was transferred from the high pressure upper cylinders to the low pressure lower cylinders. *Above right:* A big Pacific, typically on an express run. *At right:* A mammoth 2-8-8-4 freight engine in action.

first decade of this century. These were fast passenger engines (a Pennsy Atlantic had hit 127.1 mph in 1905), with 78 or 80 inch drivers and weighing 75–100 tons. However, with the B&O decision to replace its wooden passenger cars with passenger cars of steel, President Willard saw that more powerful engines would be required.

The Pacific type locomotive was the obvious answer, with its six 74-inch drivers and 144 tons of locomotive iron. A few had been ordered as early as 1906, by B&O President Murray, and between 1911 and 1917, President Willard had ordered 80 more from the Baldwin Works, and 30 more Pacifics had been provided by the United States Railroad Administration in 1919. President Willard ordered more Pacifics from Baldwin in 1922, and in 1927 ordered 20 more from Baldwin, but these particular locomotives were destined to be named for US Presidents Washington through Arthur, with but one *President Adams*, to honor both of the executives having that name. With special olive green-trimmed-with-gold paint jobs, these were sleek, fast and efficient engines—each having drivers of 80 inches and 50,000 lb of tractive force. A 21st presidential special was added to the list in 1928, this being the *President Cleveland*.

The Diesel on the Horizon

From the 1920s until the diesel era, the B&O passenger engine of choice was the 4-6-2 Pacific. While the actual number of B&O locomotives declined by 274 units from 1920–29, the tractive power per engine average increased by 10,000 lb in that same period, so, the B&O was trimming its locomotive fleet down, but the revamped fleet was far more efficient than the old—economically, a sound tradeoff in anyone's book.

The twentieth century saw the very apex of steam power, with engines cranking out more tractive force per pound than ever before. The engines themselves were bigger, and more sophisticated. Yet, the twentieth century was the age of dieselization.

The B&O's first diesel was a 60 ton, 300 hp switcher, bought for East coast yard work in 1925. The years 1930–40 saw an increase of diesels on the B&O. That decade featured the fewest locomotives purchased in several decades—some 44 locomotives—seven steam engines and 37 diesels!

The steamers bought in this period were nothing to snort at, of course: they included two mallets, a 4-6-4 Hudson type named the *Lord Baltimore*, and an experimental 4-4-4-4 engine named for the then Chief of Motive Power and Equipment, George H Emerson. The *George H Emerson* was built as a passenger hauler in 1937, and with its eight 76-inch drivers and 65,000 lb of tractive force, this mighty four cylinder could pull the heaviest passenger trains at high speeds with ease.

The B&O bought its first road diesel in 1935, for use with its newly inaugurated air conditioned, streamlined passenger trains. This diesel replaced the *Lord Baltimore*

Above far left: The B&O's 4-6-2 Pacific *President Washington*, at the B&O Museum in 1982. *At far left:* This diesel was bought in 1935 for the B&O's very own *Royal Blue* passenger express. *Below:* A streamlined Pacific heads west with the *Cincinnatian* in 1948.

on the Washington-New York *Royal Blue* passenger streamliner run, with a streamlined Pacific type steamer making the alternate runs on the line. This diesel was a two unit engine, and it worked out so well that the B&O bought two more diesel-powered streamliners (complete trains) to operate its Washington-Chicago *Capitol Limited* service. The other diesels bought in the 1930s were yard switchers.

The largest steam locomotives bought from 1940–45 were without a doubt, the 30 giant, articulated Baldwin M-1s. These were 2-8-8-4 locos delivering 115,000 lb of tractive force via their 16 64-inch drivers. Each engine with tender weighed over one million pounds. And 20 of the faithful Mikados were converetd by the Mount Clare Shops into Mountain type 2-8-2s.

Also during the war years, dieselization continued. Of the B&O's 150 new locomotives bought then, 40 percent were diesels, and of these, there were nine passenger units, several road freight units and many yard switchers. The road frieght units were 5400 hp four-unit locomotives. B&O was one of the first eastern lines to use diesels for road freight service.

A New Era

The diesel had many advantages over the steam engine —it could go farther for less cost, it was pound-for-pound more powerful, it was dependable and easily maintained, it could reverse its engines to aid braking, its low center of gravity allowed greater speed on curves, it developed high horsepower at low speed (thus cutting the time it took to make headway), and, while each diesel was expensive to buy, its dependability and good economy more than made up for the cost of purchase— and it did not consume the large quantities of water that steam engines did, thus allowing the discarding of expensive-to-maintain tank facilities.

In 1945, B&O steam units outnumbered diesels by 15 to one. In 1958, B&O President Simpson proclaimed that the B&O was using diesels for all operations, and by year's end of 1960, there were 1129 diesels on the B&O roster, and no steam engines. The age of the diesel had come, and such companies as Alco, Baldwin and General Motors (EMC) would supply not only the B&O's motive needs, but those of the entire nation as well. Baldwin, long one of the preeminent steam locomotive builders, went into the diesel business with some success, but finally closed its doors.

The diesel era would also see further big changes in the B&O—as we, too, shall shortly see.

Below: Samuel Vauclain, President of the Baldwin Locomotive Works, poses with his family and one of he and his company's creations—a huge 2-6-6-2 locomotive, built for the B&O in the 1920s, but symbolic of the B&O's search for perfection. This century has seen the apex *and* decline of steam power. *At right:* An EMD EA 'shovel nose' diesel heads a B&O passenger train in 1945.

WORLD WAR II AND AFTER

The Second World War

By the time of Daniel Willard's death, a second but more terrifying and more devastating World War had begun in Europe. Soon, war swept over all the Earth, embroiling the United States and most of the other principal nations.

In 1939, Adolf Hitler, leader of Nazi Germany, climaxed a series of bloodless conquests by the very bloody invasion of Poland; Great Britain and France therefore declared war upon Germany. In 1940, in preparation for its own possible involvement in the conflict, the US began preparing its manpower and industrial resources. In 1941, the United States passed the Lend-Lease Act to enable it to provide arms and supplies to the nations fighting against the Axis Powers — which were then defined as Germany, Italy, Japan, Hungary, Spain and Romania. The burden upon American railroads increased as American industry poured out war materials for the nations that were soon to be our allies.

The Second World War was to demand far more than had ever before been required from American industry and American manpower. US railroads, with less equipment than had been available in the First World War, would be called upon to carry far greater loads of supplies and men.

B&O President White

The Baltimore & Ohio, along whose lines were hundreds of war plants and scores of camps and depots for the armed forces, and whose steel rails led to three of America's greatest seaports — Baltimore, New York and Philadelphia — bore a large part of the transportation burden. The man who headed the B&O during this period of turmoil and heavy duty was well-qualified for the tremendous task. This man, Roy Barton White, who took over the Presidency of the B&O in 1941, had spent many years of his career in railroading and knew the industry 'from the ground up.'

Born at Metcalf, Illinois in 1883, the son of an Illinois railroad man, Mr White learned Morse code in his early teens, and began his career as a railroad telegraph operator and agent in 1900 at Dana, Indiana, on a railroad that later became part of the B&O. He moved up through the ranks rapidly, and during World War I, was superintendent of the B&O's busy Philadelphia Division. In 1921 and 1922, he was general superintendent of the B&O's Maryland District, and from 1923 to 1926, he was general manager of the B&O's New York properties. In the latter year, he left the B&O to become senior vice president of the Central Railroad of New Jersey. Shortly thereafter, he became President of the Jersey Central, moving on to become President of the Western Union Telegraph Company in 1933.

The first years of Mr White's leadership of the B&O were critical ones for all the railroads, as well as for the nation. With greater handicaps than had prevailed during World War I, how would America's railroads bear up under the new, and greater, burden of World War II?

The United States did not declare war until Japanese aircraft attacked without warning and crippled the American naval base at Pearl Harbor, Hawaii on 7 December 1941. Transportation burdens in the US increased more sharply than ever before. American railroads had to gear themselves to the unprecedented demands of engaging in warfare on fighting fronts throughout the world. The volume of traffic they were asked to handle exceeded anything that even railroad men had thought possible.

A Crushing Burden

The railroad burden was accentuated by the transfer of coastal and intercoastal ships to transoceanic freight routes and by the sharp reduction of motor truck transportation as the result of scarcity of gasoline and rubber tires. The diversion of coastal vessels and the activities of enemy submarines that hampered shipping in general required the railroads to haul many commodities that ordinarily would have been waterborne. Chief among these was oil. During 1943, the B&O alone hauled an average of 850 oil tank cars daily. Also, bituminous coal production in 1943 reached a record high, constituting the largest single item of freight on the B&O lines. Troop movements in the US, 97 percent of which were carried by rail, swelled B&O passenger traffic to an unprecedented level.

These tasks were accomplished in spite of a shortage of rolling stock — in particular, freight cars. But heavy

Power for heavy traffic. Previous page: A 2-10-2 and train. *Below:* Consolidation 2-8-0s doublehead a freight — one way to haul heavy burdenage when you couldn't use a Mallet like the one *at right.*

industries were devoted to war production, and there was little opportunity for the building of new rolling stock, however badly it was needed.

Nevertheless, the B&O plugged away with an improvement program. From 1943 to 1946, it spent nearly $89 million for improvement, including the addition of new steam and diesel-electric locomotives to its fleet, and the improving of its right-of-way and other facilities. The B&O also began modernizing its transport communications by installing teletype machines to supplement its telegraph and telephone systems.

Railroading at the Front

Many B&O officials and employees volunteered, at the request of the War Department, to band together with representatives of 27 other railroads in providing an experienced nucleus for the 708th Railway Grand Division, a new unit of the Military Railway Service in the Army Transportation Corps.

The 708th was activated at New Orleans on 6 April 1943. In the course of a glorious career which saw it take an active part in the invasion of France and the ensuing Allied drive into the heart of Germany, the division had an *esprit de corps* for which it became famous, and which was representative of American railroad men as a whole, rather than of any particular organization.

The 708th sailed for England on 20 September 1943, and helped prepare for the invasion of Normandy. As soon as the Normandy beachhead areas were secured — in August 1944 — the railway division itself moved into France. Its job was to restore to service the European railways as quickly as they came into Allied control, so that supplies could be transported quickly to front line units. From Normandy, the 708th moved behind the advancing Allied lines from Pontanbault, France to Bad Godesburg, on the Rhine River in Germany.

The division performed magnificently throughout, and particularly during the Battle of the Bulge in December 1944. In this action, not one pound of supplies entrusted to the 708th was lost to the enemy, and the division evacuated more than 10,000 loaded freight cars from areas subsequently occupied by the Germans. The headquarters of the division remained at Liège, Belgium, even though the German counterattack came within 15 kilometers and the city was the object of a concentrated V-1 rocket bombardment.

As the war in Europe drew to a close, the 708th was required to step up its operations. Daily, an average of 35,000 tons of supplies was moved through the railroad yards of Liège. In a typical 24-hour period, the unit delivered to the fighting front some 492 cars of ammunition; 80 cars of construction rock; 16 cars of mail; 130 cars of petroleum and other oil products; 460 cars of bridge-building materials; 240 cars of coal and coke; 765 cars of rations; clothing and equipment; 89 cars of salvage material and 70 cars of water cans — a total of 2342 carloads, daily. In the same time period, the division also moved eight troop trains, two prisoner-of-war trains, three empty trains of passenger equipment, and 31 empty freight trains.

War-era equipment included 0-8-0s like that *at right*, shown in 1957, as well as diesels and the engines shown previously.

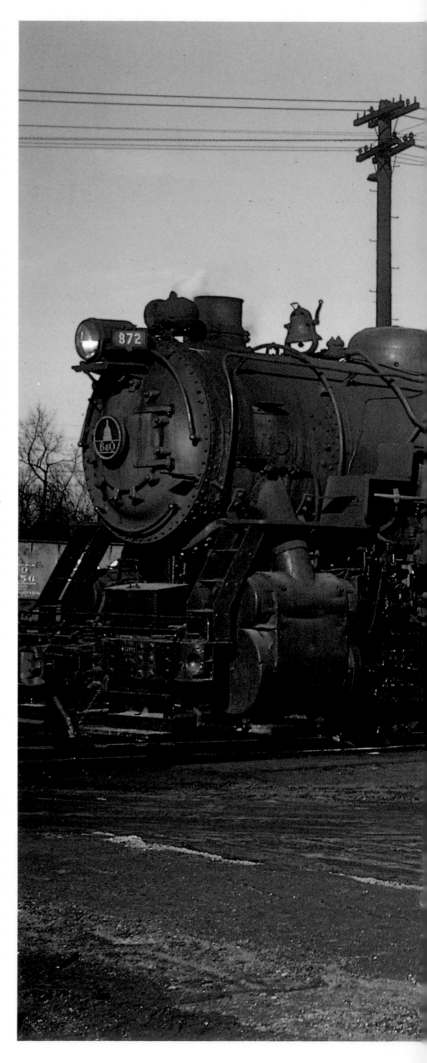

Above: This dock at Lorain, Ohio was one of the B&O's many postwar improvements. *Below left:* A B&O clearance car emerges from a tunnel in 1948. *At left:* This Mountain type 4-8-2 toppled when a rail collapsed under it in 1947 — near Hyndman, Pennsylvania.

The war over, the men of the 708th returned to their peacetime jobs in the States. Colonel WS Carr — in civilian life an officer of the New York, New Haven & Hartford Railroad — who served as Commander of the division throughout its combat career, wrote to President AB White of the B&O:

'Every B&O man in the 708th has done a marvelous job. Every one of these men has been under heavy and continuous fire many times and has carried through in a superior manner and done an outstanding job. You can well be proud of everyone.'

The War is Over

With the collapse of Germany and Japan in May and August of 1945, the decrease of wartime freight was offset by increased US exports of relief and rehabilitation supplies for the countries most damaged by the war. At the end of 1945, the railroads faced the problem of handling millions of returning service men. The wartime transport burden was not to be eased for some time after the armistice.

World War II was over; more than any other event in history, it had ushered in a new age. The atomic bombs that smashed Hiroshima and Nagasaki evidenced an unprecedentedly devastating force. World War II had damaged homes, cities, political systems, governments and people. It had severely damaged national economies as well.

Evidence of this was that the US and British railroads, with one Canadian line, were now the only major rail systems in the world not government-owned or controlled at the war's end. Further, Britain's railroads soon were to be socialized, leaving only the railroads of North America under private ownership and operation.

The tremendous war traffic had actually hurt US railroads both physically and financially. Many railroads, such as the Pennsy, found themselves with severely worn equipment and physical plants that had been greatly expanded to suit the war and were now tremendously costly excesses, badly in need of trimming at the railroads' own expense. Also, railroads — unlike most other heavy industries of the time — could not automatically raise the prices of their services to meet the increased costs of labor and materials.

Permission for rate increases first had to be obtained from the Interstate Commerce Commission, and this was a lengthy procedure — especially in light of the fact that legislation had been passed to insure that US railroads would not make high profits from war: this legislation was the federally-enacted Excess Profits Tax Law. Therefore, even with high traffic volumes after the war, railroads had to spend their money to repair physical plants that they hadn't the money to repair during the war.

The B&O Looks to the Future

Thus, in the postwar period when the American railroads were handling the greatest volume of peacetime traffic in their history, many of them had little money left over after expenses for improvements that were necessary, or for modernizations that the public desired. In the face of this, the B&O nevertheless sought to obtain new passenger and freight equipment and rebuild and expand its right-of-way.

During the war, B&O designers had dreamed about the trains they would build for postwar passenger comfort. The first postwar fruit of their imagination was the *Cincinnatian*, a coach streamliner that went into fast daylight service between Baltimore, Washington and Cincinnati in January of 1947. Four mighty Pacific type 4-6-2 streamlined steam locomotives were built to power the twin *Cincinnatians* on their daily runs. Each of the trains was made up of five 80-foot cars, including three luxurious coaches, a combination baggage-buffet-lounge and a combination diner-observation lounge.

The *Cincinnatian* was, for years, operated over the heavily traveled B&O line between Cincinnati and Detroit. In 1949, the B&O added another new passenger special — the *New Columbian*. Built by the Pullman Standard Car Manufacturing Company at a cost of nearly $2 million, this train featured the first 'strata-dome' or glass-topped observation coaches to be used on any Eastern railroad. The two eight-car sections of the *New Columbian* were placed in fast overnight service between Washington, DC and Chicago. Later, these 'strata-dome' sleeping cars were purchased for the B&O's *Capitol Limited* and its *Shenandoah*.

Many new, all-compartment sleeping cars also were purchased for the B&O's top train, the *Capitol Limited* — a Chicago-Washington-New York flyer. New coaches were built, and others were remodeled in the B&O's own shops for express trains on feature runs. Diesel-electric power for passenger service was supplemented by the purchase of new diesel locomotive units.

A postwar improvement in the B&O's freight transportation service was called 'Sentinel Service.' This provided a fast scheduled freight service from the door of the

shipper to that of the receiver. Both knew, in advance, the exact day and hour that shipments would be on hand for unloading at destination. In addition, a constant record was kept of the movement of all such freight through then state-of-the-art teletype communications. Within a year, the speed, efficiency and dependability of Sentinel Service had won acclaim from rail shippers everywhere.

Close on the heels of Sentinel Service, the B&O inaugurated another new type of fast-freight service for 'LCL,' or less-than-carload, shipments. Known as 'Time-Saver,' for wholesalers and retailers, this service provided exceptionally fast transportation over long distances. Goods that left New York on Monday evening, for example, would arrive in Chicago before dawn on the following Wednesday. Between many points, 'Time-Saver' freight runs equalled the speed of first-class passenger trains.

Communications, Improvements and Motive Power

The B&O, in cooperation with eight other railroads and five coal producing companies, fostered the development of an entirely new, but unsuccessful, type of motive power — a coal-burning gas turbine locomotive. This locomotive was expected to develop three times as much of the potential power from coal as did the ordinary steam locomotive. While some of these engines were built by various roads, they proved to be too complex and finicky for normal operation and maintenance, and the steam turbine locomotive went down in history, as did the conventional steam locomotive, as not quite as reliable as the durable and versatile diesel.

Above: These were both class P-7 Pacifics (circa 1947), but the one on the left (technically a P-7d) underwent streamlining for the B&O's *Cincinnatian* service, and the P-7 on the right didn't.

Wartime achievements in electronics enabled the B&O to install very high frequency ('VHF') two-way radios to control freight yard operations at New Castle, Pennsylvania, and at other points. Subsequently, similar equipment was installed on B&O tugs in the busy harbors of Baltimore and New York to facilitate contact with dispatchers on shore.

The B&O, in conjunction with the American Telephone and Telegraph Company, also installed public telephone service on one of its trains. This service began on the B&O's *Royal Blue* between Washington and New York. It enabled rail travelers to make business or personal calls while en route. In the hectic postwar era, America's railroads looked ahead and planned for a better future.

The men and women of the B&O, aware that the best serve themselves when they provided the best service for the public, set out under the leadership of forward-looking B&O President White to make the B&O even more efficient. Within a few years after the end of World War II, the B&O had adopted a program involving the expenditure of hundreds of millions of dollars for a large scale modernization and improvement program.

Millions of dollars went for new locomotives and new freight and passenger cars, as well as for complete new trains. Millions more went for new coal and ore docks at Lorain, Toledo, Baltimore and Staten Island; for new railroad yards at Chicago, East St Louis and Cincinnati; for right-of-way realignment and new trackage; for new bridges at Baltimore and at Point Pleasant, West Virginia. Money also went to such projects as the installation of new communications facilities throughout the B&O lines, and the building of new shops and diesel locomotive servicing facilities.

Entering the 1950s

The B&O's dieselization program moved ahead rapidly, as the diesel locomotive proved its efficiency. By the spring of 1951, the company owned more than 600 diesel locomotives. Also at this time, B&O was a system made up of some 6000 miles of road and 11,000 miles of track; approximately 2000 locomotives; almost 100,000 freight cars; and 1300 passenger cars. The system had more than 20,000 stockholders and and had assets of more than $1.2 billion.

Entering the 1950s, the B&O served 13 states with its own lines, and served many of the largest US cities and industries in the highly industrial Northeast. A vast railroad, one of the largest in the nation at that time, the B&O nevertheless had not outgrown the tradition of service that had marked its beginning and had distinguished it for well over 120 years. From its early years, it had been known as 'The Railroad University of America.' It had come to be a mainstay for the many millions of people who depended upon it daily for the efficient and regular delivery of all the things that make modern living possible.

There had, however, been increasingly voluminous incursions upon regular railroad carriage — of passengers and freight — by the automobile, the tractor trailer and the airplane. Not only that, but the US government was aligning itself decidedly with these latter, and, in terms of economic aid and needed legislation, would soon leave the nation's railroads high and dry in the economically unstable 1950s. Hard times were ahead.

Hard Times, Indeed

In the months following the war, the intensive traffic on the B&O quickly ceased. Freight revenue fell 14 percent in 1946, and passenger revenue dropped 25 percent. Expenses exceeded earnings by over half a million dollars. Inflation was a bugaboo, too, as the consumer price index rose by almost 90 percent in the postwar years. Payroll, fuel, materials and supply costs had all risen by over 100 percent in the 1940s. While total dollar revenues were to assume promising proportions in the postwar years, these figures were deceptive, as they were the products of an inflated economy — inflated prices, fares and profits.

Even so, sixteen new passenger cars were put into service as the *Columbian*, which ran between Washington and Chicago and featured a vista dome car, and passenger-viewable instruments including a clock, an altimeter, a barometer and a speedometer. Passenger cars were rebuilt for the new daylight flyer between Washington and Cincinnati. This new service was christened the *Cincinnatian*, and was inaugurated on 7 January 1947, and yet, as an indication of the dismal postwar passenger traffic situation, the *Cincinnatian* was shifted to a Cincinnati-Detroit route in 1950.

The automobile and the motor truck were biting into railroad revenues in other ways, too. In 1948, the nation's railroads expended $1.7 billion for maintenance and upkeep of their physical plants. All of this was railroad money — none of it was subsidized. By comparison, the US government spent $2.7 billion to build the public highways upon which the railroads' competition rode. Adding to the irony was the fact that the railroads themselves had provided much of the highway money, too — through payment of taxes.

By the early 1950s, passenger service deficits were staggering. On the freight side of things, however, the haulage was much the same as it had always been, and higher post-World War II freight rates, and a modest freight increase during the Korean War helped to keep things profitable. However, 47.5 percent of the total net

Part of the B&O improvements program was the upgrading of rolling stock. *Below:* On the left, an advanced steam design meant to compete (a futile attempt) with such as the EMD diesel on the right.

Postwar power. *At left:* An EMD F3 diesel moves the *Columbian* across the Thomas Viaduct (also see caption, page 26). Durable, but worn — a 1953 EMD F7 *(above)*, in 1964. *At far left:* This EMD EA (now at the B&O Museum) served both during and after the war.

freight income during that period went toward plugging the enormous financial leak created by the aforementioned passenger service deficits.

In sad truth, however, the first serious bite had occurred way back in the Great Depression, when many railroads were in the position of having to operate on what was termed 'funded debt.' This meant, roughly, that debts were guaranteed, and the railroads' own payments on them were deferred until a later time when they would be paid with interest. Daniel Willard had managed to kill off a good chunk of the B&O's funded debt in 1941, but there were still notes to pay. The terrible fact that, since 1930, there hadn't been a railroad passenger line in the country that actually made money, didn't help matters at all.

In 1944 occurred what was to be popularly dubbed 'the B&O bankruptcy of 1944.' More than $112 million in debts, plus interest, came due for the B&O that year. B&O management proposed a plan to defer the debts, setting their new maturity dates between 1965 and 2010. Though the plan was set up under the Chapter XV of the Bankruptcy Act, the railroad had never actually been on the brink of receivership.

It took two years for the ICC and the federal courts to approve the payment setup, but they did. This somewhat lightened, but did not remove, the burden of debt that weighed on the railroad, and postwar traffic revenue problems would exacerbate this situation.

Labor problems added to wage costs. All in all, the postwar period was not comfortable for the railroads.

THE B&O, THE C&O AND CSX CORPORATION

The Foreboding 1950s

Howard Simpson succeeded Roy White as President of the B&O in 1953, when operating revenues topped $460 million. President Simpson's Annual Report cited the year as 'one of the best in the history' of the B&O. However, revenues were to sink to 25 percent less than the 1953 figure by 1961, while operating expenses remained relatively constant. Net income after fixed charges shrank from its $28 million 1953 level to less than nothing in 1963, a bad deficit year.

The percentage of all US intercity freight hauled by railroads dropped from 56 percent to 43 percent in the 1950s. Even so, the B&O spent well over $200 million for property improvements during the 1950s, with much of the money going to new equipment, in particular, new diesel engines and over 10,000 freight cars.

Passenger revenues dropped from $21 million in 1953 to $21 million in 1961. Airlines and private autos accounted for much of this decline. In fact, the private auto was by far the single most popular mode of transportation of the period. The General Motors Company and automakers in general were slaying the mighty and magnificent rail passenger giant with commercial slogans like 'See the USA in your Chevrolet.'

Howard Simpson was not easily discouraged, however. A passenger traffic man 'from way back,' in 1954 he upgraded the *Capitol Limited*, the *National Limited* and the *Diplomat* with 11 new duplex roomette-bedroom sleepers that were bought from the Budd company. Additionally, Rail Diesel Cars were used on some lines in passeneger haulage, and additional improvements in the form of 'slumbercoaches,' which provided low-cost sleeping accomodation for coach passengers, were added to some trains in the mid-to-late 1950s.

However, one had only to read the handwriting on the wall. Within the first seven years of the 1950s, more than 100 B&O passenger trains were eliminated due to low traffic.

The Future Beckons

Automation was also big news during the 1950s. Centralized traffic control centers were installed in areas of heavy traffic, and automatic warning devices were installed at grade crossings. Such moves, plus the elimination of firemen from diesel locomotives, helped to trim the number of employees by 81 percent over eight years, a decline that was also a hallmark of the instability of the freight traffic during those years. Conversely, wages per employee rose 45 percent in that same period.

In the realm of improvements, new diesel fuel oil facilities were installed in Maryland, West Virginia, Ohio and Indiana. A new passenger station at Pittsburgh, ironically made necessary by the building of a highway there, and a massive bridge at Staten Island's Arthur Kill, were among the major improvements made in the late 1950s. The bridge was quite a spectacular achievement, being the world's longest vertical lift (to allow the passage of marine traffic on the Arthur Kill) railroad bridge, and since it was a boon to navigation on the aforementioned stretch of water, the US government assumed 90 percent of its construction costs.

Along with all the other changes of the 1960s, the B&O replaced its passenger and freight color schemes. Compare the EMD E9 passenger diesel of 1962 *on the previous page* with the passenger diesel shown *at top, above*, of 1968. *At right:* An all-Royal Blue EMD F7 freight diesel of the late 1960s (compare with photos on pages 122 and 124). *Above:* A tug, named for B&O President White, in 1978—by which time the B&O had undergone great change.

Automated track laying and maintenance machines cut down on the track gang force, and television cameras installed in the Potomac Yard in Washington eliminated workers who had been engaged for the purpose of car identification. New freight service, some of which has been covered in our chapter on the postwar years, offered a glimmer of hope in the increasingly dismal financial picture that was formed by the B&O's late 1950s operations. Almost 300 trailers and over 200 flat cars had been assigned to 'piggyback' service. The annual revenues

from this service rose from half a million dollars in 1955 to $6.6 million in 1961. However, that year, expenses were almost 87 percent of earnings.

Critics of the nation's railroads, especially the 'big three' eastern roads — the NYC, the Pennsy and the B&O — said that, while roads like the C&O had benefitted from aggressive management policies, the B&O, NYC and Pennsy were suffering from unaggressive management policies. A saving grace in the increasingly torpid B&O financial atmosphere was the relatively low amount of excess trackage and equipment on the B&O. As the NYC and the Pennsy were rapidly finding, the extravagant building that was done to handle World War II traffic left those two roads with costly, elephantine physical plants that acted very much like anchors in dragging both roads to the murky depths of red ink.

The B&O was suffering from low traffic, a common railroad blight in the 1950s–60s. The year 1961 was a crushing blow for the B&O — with only $2.6 million of net income for the year, after taxes, rents and fixed charges, the B&O came up $31 million short. This would be a catastrophic situation in any industry, but again, fortune wryly smiled upon the B&O.

A Takeover in the Nick of Time

As we have said, the B&O was in terrible financial shape in the late 1950s–early 1960s. Many roads were hurting in the 1950s. New modes of transportation had even put a dent in the freight business. The nation's small railroads were engaged in a veritable merger fever that only increased as the decade drew to a close. The larger railroads—especially the eastern roads—took note of this.

The New York Central was reeling under the unstable fortunes of the industrial northeast, as was its chief competitor, the giant Pennsylvania Railroad. These two, naturally, sought the bittersweet solace of merger, as they were both sinking fast. They were a bit evasive about the idea at first, for the NYC feared a merger in which the Pennsy would attempt to squash it. (It was an intense and old rivalry, the NYC's fears were, in fact, eventually realized, with dire results for both entities).

In one of its more intricate steps, the NYC cast its merger-filled eyes upon the Chesapeake & Ohio and the B&O: no threat of being taken over wholesale there! Cyrus Eaton and Walter Tuohy, the owner and the President of the C&O, respectively, felt that the NYC's financial situation was so bad that only *after* a merger of the C&O and the B&O would they consider a merger with the NYC. By 1960, the C&O had applied to the ICC for permission to purchase a majority share of the B&O common stock. B&O President Howard Simpson wanted to hold out for a direct, three-way merger, with control of the newly merged road shared by the leadership of the three pre-existing lines.

C&O Control, and Merger

In 1961, President Tuohy of the C&O announced that the C&O had definitely gained control of 61 percent of the B&O common stock. This effectively told President Simpson that the cards—all of them—were in the hands of the C&O. At the regular Board of Directors meeting on 17 May 1961, Jervis Langdon, Jr was elected President, and former President Simpson was made Chairman of the Board and Chief Executive Officer.

Before the merger could be made official, the approval of the Interstate Commerce Commission was needed. The US government had long been alert to the danger of common carrier monopolies, and the ICC was the chief 'watchdog' for that kind of thing. Therefore, all mergers involving railroads, as well as other large transport entities, had to submit to the approval of the ICC. That of course meant having hearings, so that all parties that were for the merger, as well as all parties that were against the merger, could present their points of view.

By now, the B&O was in terrible shape. Maintenance had been deferred for several years to defray costs, and freight service was starting to suffer. The C&O, on the other hand, originated more coal traffic than any other US railroad, and as such, was snugly ensconced in a position of control as the hauler of the one commodity than no other means of transportation—save barges and ships—could haul in quantity with anything even approaching a reasonable economy.

The Chesapeake & Ohio had its beginnings in the Louisa Railroad, a central Virginia short line chartered in 1836. By 1850, the little road had stretched its trackage to Richmond, and changed its name to 'The Virginia

Central Railroad' and grew into a line that stretched from Richmond through Gordonsville, Charlottesville and Staunton to Jackson's River. Though it was ravaged by the Civil War, the road's plucky managers nevertheless changed its name to 'The Chesapeake & Ohio Railroad' and procured financing for an extension to the Ohio River. Though it suffered setbacks, by the turn of the century the C&O was a prosperous, 1445-mile line from Newport News, Virginia to Cincinnati and Louisville — and was seriously competing with the B&O for West Virginia coal.

Financial control of the C&O seemed to go from one set of hands to another in the twentieth century — first it was the Pennsylvania Railroad and the New York Central Railroad, then the Van Swerigen brothers, then Robert Young and his Allegheny Corporation, and finally, in 1954, Cyrus Eaton. By this time, the C&O was a 5000-mile railroad with annual revenues of $350 million; an incredibly good coal traffic; diversified freight traffic (as a result of a 1947 buyout of the Pere Marquette Railroad); and the virtuoso leadership of Walter J Tuohy, the C&O President since 1948. Now, in the early 1960s, the promise of a B&O merger was yet another opportunity.

C&O President Walter Tuohy was a dynamic, energetic and intelligent man, whose policies had made the C&O

an efficient, high-grossing operation in an era when most American railroads were merging to save their lives. President Tuohy was in the position to call the shots, and he certainly did. In the case of the newly-acquired B&O, he had extremely capable help in the person of President Langdon, who managed to cut expenses and actually raise the B&O's revenue in 1962. The road had a net income of $1.6 million that year, as compared to 1961 with its monstrous deficit.

Meanwhile, ICC approval of the merger was in process. It had been pointed out by both B&O and C&O management that the B&O and C&O were complementary lines, rather than competitive, and that the stronger road could help pull the weaker one up. Not only that, unification was seen as a brake against the B&O's slide toward bankruptcy. Besides, the C&O was willing to spend $250 million over five years to revamp the sagging B&O.

The desperate NYC, doing what it could to forestall a merger with the ailing Pennsy, still hoped to merge with the B&O, and fought hard against the B&O/C&O merger, saying that such a merger would in fact result in further losses for the B&O. The NYC also expressed its fears that such a combined system would drain millions of tons of freight from NYC routes, but, in the end, the merger prevailed, and the NYC went to its fate with the Pennsy, in the Penn Central fiasco. This latter tale did have a happy ending in the eventual formation of the Conrail system.

In the age of merger. *Below left:* An Alco FA-2 freight diesel and helper units with a B&O train in Illinois, in 1964. *Below:* An EMD road switcher, here equipped for B&O passenger service in 1962.

The B&O and the C&O

Bucking the unions and most other eastern railroads, the ICC said 'Yes!' to the B&O/C&O merger on New Year's Eve, 1962. It was felt in some quarters that the resulting road would be the strongest in the East. On 4 February 1963, the C&O formalized its control over the B&O. The ceremony took place at one minute after midnight, as that was the moment that the ICC approval became official. It was fitting that the knot be tied in Baltimore, in the old B&O boardroom, redolent with the history of the nation's oldest railroad.

The combined system was composed of 11,000 miles of trackage stretching from the Atlantic Ocean to the Mississippi River, and from the Great Lakes to the southern border of Kentucky.

The B&O obtained loans from C&O financiers to enhance its ailing fleet. Facilities were also refurbished, tunnels enlarged and freight yards were upgraded. In March 1968, the ICC approved the acquisition of the Western Maryland Railway by the B&O/C&O, and this 800-mile line became part of the system.

Over the years, C&O men slowly but surely replaced the B&O men on the B&O executive board. In 1964, Jervis Langdon left the B&O Presidency for the Presidency of the Rock Island Lines. Walter Tuohy was then elected President of the B&O, and upon his death in 1966, Gregory DeVine stepped into his twin Presidencies on the B&O and C&O. By 1970, the B&O Board included six men that were also on the C&O Board; 1970 also marked the 94th percentile in C&O holdings of B&O common stock.

The End of the Passenger Era

The B&O's passenger service had been a losing proposition for decades, and many passenger lines had already been cut. Yet, while passenger traffic on every interurban railroad in the nation was terrible, some rail passenger service was still needed. Therefore, the federal government had not allowed major interurban carriers such as the B&O to simply discontinue passenger service, even though such service was responsible for stupendous losses. Called on for a practical solution, the government created the National Railroad Passenger Corporation, aka 'Amtrak,' in 1970. Amtrak trains would use existing trackage but would be federally run. All the B&O was required to do in order to put its passenger traffic to rest was to make a one-time only payment of $29.6 million to the National Railroad Passenger Corporation. Thus freed, the road concentrated its energies on freight.

Hays Watkins and the Chessie System

In 1971, President DeVine retired, and was replaced by the energetic Hays Watkins, a C&O man since 1949. President Watkins had the appellation 'Chessie System' adopted as a marketing name for the C&O/B&O and Western Maryland conglomerate. The name 'Chessie' had an interesting history in and of itself—but more on that in a moment. The C&O and B&O continued to operate separately, even though they had a common 'head' in the Chessie System offices in Cleveland.

The name 'Chessie' obviously refers to the Chesapeake and Ohio Railroad, but in the sense in which the

As did the C&O, the B&O had a full selection of diesel power. *At top left:* An Alco GP-30 road switcher leads a trio of diesels in the early 1960s. Note the short-lived 'rising sun' paint scheme on this engine's nose (see also page 122 photo). *At top, above:* An Alco RSD-12 road switcher in 1970, in Fairmont, Virginia. *Above, middle:* A rare 1969 photo of a Baldwin AS-16 road switcher of the 'high hood' type manufactured from 1953–55. The B&O continued to operate as an entity even with the advent of the Chessie System in 1971. *Above:* Wearing the Chessie System colors in 1974, this Alco S-4 also wore the letters 'B&O.'

company uses and has used it, the name was first applied to a painting which portrayed a kitten asleep on a pillow, with a little blanket drawn up around its chin. In the early 1930s, Lionel Probert, the C&O's Assistant to the President, saw the artwork, and thought it would be an ideal advertising gimmick to emphasize the smoothness of passenger travel on the C&O. In 1933, the C&O sponsored an ad in *Fortune* magazine which included the kitten picture and the tag line 'Sleep Like a Kitten.'

The kitten proved to be an immensely popular symbol, and 'Chessie' went on to an illustrious, extended career, selling war bonds during World War II, and, when the airplane and the automobile usurped the C&O's passenger traffic, Chessie sold freight haulage, with the slogan 'Purr-fect Transportation.'

For a while, management sought to give Chessie a playmate, by way of emphasizing the unification of C&O and B&O operations. This little kitty was to be known as 'Bessie' (for obvious reasons) but, after a survey of the shareholders brought forth almost no response to the idea, Bessie was erased from the promotional department's drawing boards. The Chessie System logo, 'Chessie' in silhouette within a 'C' shape, appeared on the equipment of the Chessie System's lines.

The B&O was in the process of absorbing the Western Maryland's operations, and eventually completely absorbed the WM. In 1974, Cyrus Eaton gave up his Board chairmanship, and Hays Watkins became President and Chairman of the Chessie System.

A B&O Sesquicentennial

The nation's common carrier railroad, the B&O celebrated its 150th birthday on 28 February 1977. Hays Watkins organized a celebration of 350 guests at the B&O Railroad Museum in Baltimore. Featured events included a staged race between the *Tom Thumb* and the *Best Friend of Charleston*, and dinner, including a huge white birthday cake (baked at the Chessie System's Greenbriar Resort Hotel), amidst the engines and cars in the museum's roundhouse. A short while later, to continue the celebratory mood, the annual shareholder's meeting was held in the same venue.

The 150th Anniversary year also saw the sales of 'Sesquicentennial Special' blue china plates bearing the image of Charles Carroll laying the historic 'first stone of the B&O' way back on 4 July 1828. Chessie System steam specials were available for round trip and one way trips from a number of cities in eight states. All in all, it was a grand celebration of the railroad that had grown up with the country itself.

It was a good sesquicentennial decade for the B&O. By 1979, when John Collinson became President of the B&O, total operating revenues for the Chessie System had risen by more than $800 million since the beginning of the 1970s. Net earnings had increased by over $85 million, with an inflationary skew. However, inflation or no, there had been a two-for-one stock split back in 1974, and the price of the split shares rose on top of that, showing that the foundation of the system was going strong in a time of turmoil for many other railroads, proving that early predictions concerning the strength of the B&O/C&O merger were correct.

CSX Corporation

In the latter half of 1980, the ICC approved a merger of the Chessie System with the Seaboard Coast Line (later, the Seaboard System). The Seaboard Coast Line had its origins in mid-1967, when the Atlantic Coast Line and the Seaboard Air Line merged. A little later, the Piedmont & Northern, and the Durham & Southern railroads were brought in. The affiliated Louisville & Nashville Railroad was operated independently, even though it was, as the Seaboard Coast Lines company literature of the 1970s put it, one of the 'The Family Lines,' meaning it was at least part of the SCL marketing operation.

At left: In this 1972 photo, Chessie the sleeping kitten rides the nose of an EMD GP40 road switcher. Once symbolic of passenger comfort, Chessie here stood for 'Purr-fect Transportation.' Upon merger with Seaboard Coast Lines in 1980, the paint scheme changed again to proclaim the resultant CSX Corporation. Into the future—*below, below bottom and below left:* These EMD GP40s wear the CSX colors *plus* the historic, identifying initials of the B&O.

The merger of the Chessie System and the Seaboard Coast Line on 1 November 1980 produced a holding company for the two large systems which was known as the CSX Corporation. Prime Osborn III, of Seaboard, became Chairman, and Hays Watkins was elected President of the new entity. Press hype had it that the C stood for Chessie, the S for Seaboard and the X for the fact that the system was much larger than the simple addition of one system to another.

At this point, the B&O represented one-fifth the mileage, revenue and work force of the parent organization. As for the CSX Corporation, with whom the B&O's future is inextricably linked, the Chessie System kept its headquarters in Cleveland, and Seaboard remained based in Jacksonville, Florida. CSX set up its headquarters in Richmond, Virginia. As of last report, CSX had 70,000 employees, 27,000 miles of railroad, assets in excess of $7.5 billion and a physical plant that accessed 22 states. In May 1982, Prime Osborn III retired and Hays Watkins succeeded him as Chairman.

Its total revenues of nearly five billion dollars included earnings from large real estate holdings of coal, oil and gas. John Collinson was President of the B&O from 1979 −83, and was succeeded by JW Snow.

The L&N was eventually fully merged into the SCL organization in December of 1982, to create the Seaboard System Railroad, Incorporated, which was altogether composed of (in addition to the above-named roads) the Clinchfield Railroad, the Georgia Railroad, the Western Railway of Alabama, the Atlanta & West Point Railroad and the Newberry & Laurens Railroad.

The Chessie System itself operates more than 50,000 freight cars over more than 11,000 miles of track. CSX is the nation's largest coal hauler. It is estimated that the combined operation saves nearly 15 million gallons of fuel annuallly through combined and cooperative operations. In 1983, CSX Corporation and Texas Gas announced a definitive agreement for the combination of operations, and the same year, CSX Corporation also established a voting trust—subject to ICC approval—for the Commercial Barge Line Company. Progress continued apace; in 1984, CSX Corporation and Southern New England Telephone entered upon a cooperative agreement for 'Lightnet' fiber optic communications system construction and testing.

In 1985, CSX Corporation realigned itself into four major divisions—Transportation, Technology, Energy and Properties. An offer to purchase the Sea-Land container operation was tendered in 1986, and that same year, Seaboard System Railroad, Incorporated underwent a name change to CSX Transportation, Incorporated. C&O and B&O continued to exist as separate entities, although some of their business was to be conducted through CSX Transportation on an agency basis. In the latter part of that year, B&O, C&O and CSX Tranportation Incorporated consolidated into one corporation.

So there it is, the continually unfolding story of the nation's oldest common carrier railroad—through good times and bad, continually meeting the challenge. Today, CSX, and within it, the B&O, face the 1990s and a world that needs efficient, knowledgeable service just as it did when Charles Carroll said a prayer, picked up his spade and turned the first shovelful of earth for the 'first stone' of the historic Baltimore & Ohio Railroad.

INDEX